On Eagles' Wings

Thematic Prayer, Meditation,
And Services Of The Word
For Christian Burial

Gail Gaymer Martin

CSS Publishing Company, Inc., Lima, Ohio

For more information about CSS Publishing Company resources, visit our website at www.csspub.com.

ISBN 0-7880-1796-9

To the memory of Dominic Mastri
with special thanks to his family
who inspired this book.

Table Of Contents

Preface

The death of a loved one is a time of decision-making. Church staff, whether clergy or lay leaders, and families find it necessary to make many decisions offering a multitude of choices. While the family is faced with logistical details of the funeral visitation and burial, the clergy or church lay leaders are contacted to offer words of comfort and hope, as well as prepare and select the texts for the funeral service and/or the prayer service at the funeral home. All of these decisions must be made within a short time frame.

Questions arise regarding the style of prayer service or funeral service, the service theme, and the particular Bible verses to be used. Families do not have the luxury of time to read and study the verses to select those they feel are most appropriate for their loved ones. Under stress, lay leaders or clergy are often given the responsibility to select the readings and Bible text. The theme summary pages may be used to assist the family or church workers in making their selections.

This book of services will help to alleviate some of the stress for all concerned. Thematic services of the Word, prayer, and meditation are prepared in their entirety. A special sheet is included for duplication to be distributed to the mourners for the responsive readings and prayers. Each service is accompanied by a brief explanation as to the theme and its approach. The services are planned with opportunities for family input and may include additions such as music or special readings of poetry or favorite Bible verses that could be presented by loved ones. This book is an aid to clergy and church lay leaders, as well as the grieving family.

Introduction

This book provides services of the Word, prayer, and meditation written in a thematic style. Each may be used as a funeral home prayer service or, with simple additions, the funeral service. The services are designed to be used by two individuals, clergy and/or lay leaders. If there is a single leader, all parts, specified as **Reader** and **Leader**, would be read by one individual. If family members choose to participate, the portion of scripture assigned to the Reader may be read by one or more individuals. The name of the deceased is inserted on the blank line, as indicated. All Bible verses are taken from *The New Revised Standard Version* unless otherwise noted.

A selection of Bible verses is in the format of responsive readings. These portions of the service are prepared in a separate format following each service which can be duplicated and distributed to the participants. The responsive readings may be read by clergy or a lay leader, if preferred.

The services include two opportunities for meditation. One period of silence is for meditation on the Word of God. A second is designated as a time to reflect upon the life of the deceased. Following the second meditation, an opportunity is provided for family and friends to speak aloud and reflect upon the life of their loved one. The amount of time designated for eulogizing will be regulated by the leader. The eulogy may be deleted from the service, or it may be replaced by a sermon or eulogy from the clergy.

These services may be adapted to the needs and desires of the clergy or the family by adding music, selected readings from the Bible, poetry, or other personal traditions.

Service Theme Summary

Service 1 — The Lord Is My Shepherd

The Lord is my shepherd, I shall not want, and I shall dwell in the house of the Lord my whole life long (Psalm 23:1, 6). A shepherd knows his sheep, and he guides and cares for them. Likewise, the Good Shepherd, our Savior, protects, guides, and gave his life to assure us of salvation. This service provides comfort, and the knowledge that we are protected and guided by the loving Shepherd and that when life ends, he carries us in his arms to live with all the saints in heaven.

Service 2 — You Are A New Creation

So if anyone is in Christ, there is a new creation, everything old has passed away; see, everything has become new! (Corinthians 5:17). The Bible assures us that, as believers, our "old self" was crucified with Christ, and we walk in newness of life. As Christ died and rose again, so we are assured of our resurrection and will live in newness of life in heaven with God and with all those who have gone on before us.

Service 3 — On Eagles' Wings

The Bible tells us, *Those who wait for the Lord shall renew their strength, they shall mount up with wings like eagles, they shall run and not be weary, they shall walk and not faint* (Isaiah 40:31). This service reminds us of the strength and might of God who, like an eagle caring for its young, watches over us. We are assured God's love is steadfast from everlasting to everlasting. When our last day arrives, we will be raised on eagles' wings and carried to heaven safely in God's hands.

Service 4 — The Gift Of Life

For the wages of sin is death, but the free gift of God is eternal life in Christ Jesus our Lord (Romans 6:23). God, our creator, gave us life and planned for our salvation by giving us Jesus Christ, God's Son, as our Savior. Therefore, sin has no power over us and we are assured of the gift of eternal life in heaven.

Service 5 — I Am The Resurrection

I am the resurrection and the life. Those who believe in me, even though they die, will live, and everyone who lives and believes in me will never die (John 11:25). Before the world was made, God, our Father, provided a plan for our salvation. Adam and Eve's sin is conquered. We are victorious over death. As children of God, we are joint heirs with Christ whose death and resurrection assures us of eternal life in heaven.

Service 6 — In My Father's House

In my Father's house there are many dwelling places. If it were not so, would I have told you that I go to prepare a place for you? And if I go and prepare a place for you, I will come again and will take you to myself, so that where I am, there you may be also (John 14:2-3). Jesus assures us that God has a special place for us in heaven. Knowing that we will live with God eternally, we receive hope, comfort, and a peace which the world cannot give.

Service 7 — I Am The Bread Of Life

I am the bread of life. Whoever comes to me will never be hungry, and whoever believes in me will never be thirsty. This is the will of him who sent me, that I should lose nothing of all that he has given me, but raise it up on the last day (John 6:35, 39). God nourishes our bodies and our souls. To the Israelites, God gave manna, bread from heaven, and continues to provide us each day with our daily bread. God also gave us our Bread of Life, Jesus Christ, whose death and resurrection assures us of an eternal place in heaven.

Service 8 — I Am The True Vine

I am the vine, you are the branches (John 5:5). *You have been born anew, not of perishable but of imperishable seed, through the living and enduring word of God. "All flesh is like grass and all its glory like the flower of grass. The grass withers, and the flower falls, but the word of the Lord endures forever"* (1 Peter 1:23-25). Though human life is fragile and perishable, God has given us an imperishable life through Jesus. Like a living plant, we are watered by the Word and nourished by the Light of the Son.

Service 9 — Child Of God, Heir To The Kingdom

"Abba Father!" So you are no longer a slave but a child, and if a child then also an heir, through God (Galatians 4:6-7). We are God's children and, through Christ, we have become heirs to the kingdom of heaven. Like a loving Father, God nurtures us, guides us, and protects us, and most importantly, offers us an eternal home in heaven.

Service 10 — Our Wounds Are Healed

He himself bore our sins in his body on the cross, so that, free from sins, we might live for righteousness; by his wounds you have been healed (1 Peter 2:24). God has provided healing for our earthly body and our spiritual body. While Jesus, the Great Healer, walked the earth, he healed the sick and raised the dead. Through the sacrifice on the cross, we, too, receive forgiveness of sins and are raised from death to a newness of life, a body made perfect in heaven.

13

The Lord Is My Shepherd

(Family and friends are called to silence for the opening of the prayer service.)

Opening Invocation

Leader: We begin in the name of the Father and of the Son and of the Holy Spirit. Amen. Today we celebrate the victory of _____ who has overcome death and lives today in eternity. We remember the Lord's promises, and we receive hope and comfort for those who remain behind, waiting for the day when we, too, will be carried by the Good Shepherd to our home in heaven to be with God and all the saints where we will again see _____ face to face.

Responsive Reading from Isaiah 25:8-9

Leader: The Lord God will wipe away the tears from all faces. This is our God; we have waited for him, so that he might save us.

Response: This is the Lord for whom we have waited; let us be glad and rejoice in his salvation.

Prayer

Leader: Let us pray. Heavenly Father, you have indeed promised to dry our tears. You have given us your Son, the Good Shepherd, who has won for us the victory over death and promises us life eternal for those who believe. Heavenly Father, you have provided a Comforter, the Holy Spirit, for those who mourn. Open our hearts today to your Word, so that we may find the hope and comfort that you give us. We pray this in the name of the Good Shepherd, our Lord Jesus Christ. Amen.

Old Testament Responsive Reading

Leader: From the beginning, God has guided us like a shepherd. Listen to our Heavenly Father's words in Ezekiel 34:15-24:

Reader: I myself will be the shepherd of my sheep, and I will make them lie down, says the Lord God.

Response: I will seek the lost, and I will bring back the strayed, and I will bind up the injured, and I will strengthen the weak.

Reader: I will save my flock, and they shall no longer be ravaged; and I will judge between sheep and sheep.

Response: I will set up over them one shepherd, my servant David, and he shall feed them: he shall feed them and be their shepherd.

Reader: And I, the Lord, will be their God, and my servant David shall be prince among them; I, the Lord, have spoken.

New Testament Readings

Leader: What does it mean that the Lord is our Shepherd? It means he guides us to safety and willingly lays down his life for us. We read in Matthew 18:12-14:

What do you think? If a shepherd has a hundred sheep, and one of them has gone astray, does he not leave the ninety-nine on the mountains and go in search of the one that went astray? And if he finds it, truly I tell you, he rejoices over it more than over the ninety-nine that never went astray. So it is not the will of your Father in heaven that one of these little ones should be lost.

Reader: Jesus, himself, tells us in John 10:11-18:

I am the good shepherd. The good shepherd lays down his life for the sheep. The hired hand, who is not the shepherd and does not own the sheep, sees the wolf coming and leaves the sheep and runs away — and the wolf snatches them and scatters them. The hired hand runs away because a hired hand does not care

16

for the sheep. I am the good shepherd. I know my own and my own know me, just as the Father knows me and I know the Father. And I lay down my life for the sheep. I have other sheep that do not belong to this fold. I must bring them also, and they will listen to my voice. So there will be one flock, one shepherd. For this reason the Father loves me, because I lay down my life in order to take it up again. No one takes it from me, but I lay it down of my own accord. I have power to lay it down, and I have power to take it up again. I have received this command from my Father.

Meditation and Prayer

Leader: The Good Shepherd laid down his life for us. Let us have a moment of silence to mediate on words that offer us comfort and promise. (*Silence*) Let us pray: Father in Heaven, we thank you for the plan you laid for us in the Garden of Eden. There you prepared for us our Savior, our Good Shepherd, who leads us from sin and Satan to life eternal. We remember the words in Isaiah:

He will feed his flock like a shepherd; he will gather the lambs in his arms, and carry them in his bosom, and gently lead the mother sheep.

We thank you and praise you for your protection and love. In Jesus' name. Amen.

Reading from the Gospel of Matthew

Reader: God, our Heavenly Father, gave us the gift of eternal life. We may ask, what have we done to deserve this? The answer is we deserve nothing but God's wrath and punishment. Yet, thanks be to God, through Christ Jesus, we are set free from sin and death. For God sent his own Son, pure and sinless, in the likeness of sinful flesh, to deal with sin. It is a free gift through the grace of our Heavenly Father. Yet as an expression of our faith and our love for God, we respond to the need of

17

others. When the disciples asked about the end, we hear Jesus' response in Matthew 25:31-46:

When the Son of Man comes in his glory, and all the angels with him, then he will sit on the throne of his glory. All the nations will be gathered before him, and he will separate people one from another as a shepherd separates the sheep from the goats, and he will put the sheep at his right hand and the goats at the left. Then the king will say to those at his right hand, "Come, you that are blessed by my Father, inherit the kingdom prepared for you from the foundation of the world; for I was hungry and you gave me food, I was thirsty and you gave me something to drink, I was a stranger and you welcomed me, I was naked and you gave me clothing, I was sick and you took care of me, I was in prison and you visited me." Then the righteous will answer him, "Lord, when was it that we saw you hungry and gave you food, or thirsty and gave you something to drink? And when was it that we saw you a stranger and welcomed you, or naked and gave you clothing? And when was it that we saw you sick or in prison and visited you?" And the king will answer them, "Truly I tell you, just as you did it to one of the least of these who are members of my family, you did it to me." Then he will say to those at his left hand, "You that are accursed, depart from me into the eternal fire prepared for the devil and his angels; for I was hungry and you gave me no food, I was thirsty and you gave me nothing to drink, I was a stranger and you did not welcome me, naked and you did not give me clothing, sick and in prison and you did not visit me." Then they also will answer, "Lord, when was it that we saw you hungry or thirsty or a stranger or naked or sick or in prison, and did not take care of you?" Then he will answer them, "Truly I tell you, just as you did not do it to one of the least of these, you did not do it to me." And these will go away into eternal punishment, but the righteous into eternal life.

Meditation

Leader:　Showing our love for God, we respond to the needs and joys of others. In silence, remember the times in your life that _____ has touched you with words of kindness, words of hope, or actions of friendship and love. (*Silence*) We would like to give the opportunity to any of the family or friends who would like to share with us today a memory that recounts a special way in which _____ touched your life.

A Time for Sharing

(*The leader will allow time for recollections.*)

Comfort for the Living

Reader:　From Revelations 7 we read:

Then one of the elders addressed me, saying, "Who are these, robed in white, and where have they come from?" I said to him, "Sir, you are the one that knows." Then he said to me, "These are they who have come out of the great ordeal; they have washed their robes and made them white in the blood of the Lamb. For this reason they are before the throne of God, and worship him day and night within his temple, and the one who is seated on the throne will shelter them. They will hunger no more, and thirst no more; the sun will not strike them, nor any scorching heat; for the Lamb at the center of the throne will be their shepherd, and he will guide them to springs of the water of life, and God will wipe away every tear from their eyes" (Revelation 7:13-17).

Responsive Reading

Leader:　There is comfort in knowing that in the Good Shepherd's arms _____ will have no pain, no sorrow, no tears, for with God there is only joy. Yet for you the living, let us find comfort in the words of Psalm 23:

19

The Lord is my shepherd, I shall not want.

Response: **He makes me lie down in green pastures; he leads me beside still waters;**

Leader: He restores my soul. He leads me in right paths for his name's sake.

Response: **Even though I walk through the darkest valley, I fear no evil; for you are with me; your rod and your staff — they comfort me.**

Leader: You prepare a table before me in the presence of my enemies; you anoint my head with oil; my cup overflows.

Response: **Surely goodness and mercy shall follow me all the days of my life, and I shall dwell in the house of the Lord my whole life long.**

Leader: Let us pray the prayer that our Lord taught us to pray.

All: **Our Father which art in heaven, hallowed be thy name. Thy kingdom come. Thy will be done in earth, as it is in heaven. Give us this day our daily bread. And forgive us our debts, as we forgive our debtors. And lead us not into temptation, but deliver us from evil: For thine is the kingdom, and the power, and the glory, for ever. Amen.**

Closing Prayer

Leader: Heavenly Father, we give you thanks and praise for your loving kindness and for the gift of eternal life. We know that _____ is safe in your keeping. We ask you to keep us all in your grace. May the Good Shepherd hold us in his arms and comfort us with the knowledge that _____ lives with you in Heaven. Someday we too will reach our home in Heaven where we will meet again all of those we love who have gone on before us. Open our hearts and minds to your Word and fill us with the peace of your promises. We ask this in the name of our Savior, Jesus Christ. Amen.

(The service is concluded.)

Service Program For Distribution

The Lord Is My Shepherd

(The participants will read from the portions of the service marked **Response** *and* **All***.)*

Opening Invocation

Responsive Reading from Isaiah 25:8-9
Leader: The Lord God will wipe away the tears from all faces. This is our God; we have waited for him, so that he might save us.
Response: **This is the Lord for whom we have waited; let us be glad and rejoice in his salvation.**

Prayer

Old Testament Responsive Reading from Ezekiel 34:15-24
Reader: I myself will be the shepherd of my sheep, and I will make them lie down, says the Lord God.
Response: **I will seek the lost, and I will bring back the strayed, and I will bind up the injured, and I will strengthen the weak.**
Reader: I will save my flock, and they shall no longer be ravaged; and I will judge between sheep and sheep.
Response: **I will set up over them one shepherd, my servant David, and he shall feed them: he shall feed them and be their shepherd.**
Reader: And I, the Lord, will be their God, and my servant David shall be prince among them; I, the Lord, have spoken.

New Testament Readings

Meditation and Prayer

Reading from the Gospel of Matthew 25:31-46

Meditation

A Time for Sharing

Comfort for the Living

Psalm 23 Responsive Reading

Leader: The Lord is my shepherd, I shall not want.

Response: He makes me lie down in green pastures; he leads me beside still waters;

Leader: He restores my soul. He leads me in right paths for his name's sake.

Response: Even though I walk through the darkest valley, I fear no evil; for you are with me; your rod and your staff — they comfort me.

Leader: You prepare a table before me in the presence of my enemies; you anoint my head with oil; my cup over-flows.

Response: Surely goodness and mercy shall follow me all the days of my life, and I shall dwell in the house of the Lord my whole life long.

The Lord's Prayer

All: **Our Father which art in heaven, hallowed be thy name. Thy kingdom come. Thy will be done in earth, as it is in heaven. Give us this day our daily bread. And forgive us our debts, as we forgive our debt-ors. And lead us not into temptation, but deliver us from evil: For thine is the kingdom, and the power, and the glory, for ever. Amen.**

Closing Prayer

Service 2

You Are A New Creation

(Family and friends are called to silence for the opening of the prayer service.)

Opening Invocation
Leader: In the name of the Father and of the Son and of the Holy Spirit. Amen.

But now is Christ risen from the dead, and become the first fruits of them that slept. For since by man came death, by man came also the resurrection of the dead. For as in Adam all die, even so in Christ shall all be made alive (1 Corinthians 15:20-22 KJV).

Today, we celebrate the new life of _____ who has overcome death through Christ and lives with God in his heavenly kingdom. We thank and praise God the Father for giving us his Son, Jesus Christ who gave his life for us and became the first fruits of them who slept.

Responsive Reading from Isaiah 42:5-10
Reader: Thus says God, the Lord, who created the heavens and stretched them out, who spread out the earth and what comes from it, who gives breath to the people upon it and spirit to those who walk in it:
Response: **I am the Lord, I have called you in righteousness, I have taken you by the hand and kept you; I have given you as a covenant to the people, a light to the nations,**
Reader: To open the eyes that are blind, to bring out the prisoners from the dungeon, from the prison those who sit in darkness.
Response: **I am the Lord, that is my name; my glory I give to no other, nor my praise to idols.**

23

Reader: See, the former things have come to pass, and new things I now declare; before they spring forth, I tell you of them.

Response: Sing to the Lord a new song, his praise from the end of the earth!

Prayer

Leader: Let us pray. Heavenly Father, we thank you for your promise of life with you in Heaven. You gave us your Son, a willing sacrifice, so that we may see the former life pass away and new things spring forth for us as we pass from this world to the next. May we ever sing your praises in thanksgiving for the unspeakable gift, your Son, in whose name we pray. Amen.

Old Testament Responsive Reading

Leader: In the beginning God planned for our salvation and provided us with steadfast love. David recalled God's promise in Psalm 119:

Reader: Let your steadfast love come to me, O Lord, your salvation according to your promise.

Response: Then I shall have an answer for those who taunt me, for I trust in your word.

Reader: Your hands have made and fashioned me; give me understanding that I may learn your commandments.

Response: Those who fear you shall see me and rejoice, because I have hoped in your word.

Leader: I know, O Lord, that your judgments are right, and that in faithfulness you have humbled me.

Response: Let your steadfast love become my comfort according to your promise to your servant.

Leader: Let your mercy come to me, that I may live; for your law is my delight.

Response: Let your steadfast love come to me, O Lord, your salvation according to your promise.

New Testament Readings

Reader: The Bible tells us of the hope we have in God's plan for salvation. God knows we struggle with our sinful nature. We read in Ephesians 4:21-24:

For surely you have heard about him and were taught in him, as truth is in Jesus. You were taught to put away your former way of life, your old self, corrupt and deluded by its lusts, and to be renewed in the spirit of your minds, and to clothe yourselves with the new self, created according to the likeness of God in true righteousness and holiness.

Yet as human beings, we sometimes fail to follow God's teachings, and we experience sin and suffering. We have God's promise, though, if we repent of our wrongdoings, a new creation is ours but we must learn to wait in patience. Romans 8:20-28 says:

For the creation was subjected to futility, not of its own will but by the will of the one who subjected it, in hope that the creation itself will be set free from its bondage to decay and will obtain the freedom of the glory of the children of God. We know that the whole creation has been groaning in labor pains until now; and not only the creation, but we ourselves, who have the first fruits of the Spirit, groan inwardly while we wait for adoption, the redemption of our bodies. For in hope we were saved. Now hope that is seen is not hope. For who hopes for what is seen? But if we hope for what we do not see, we wait for it with patience. Likewise the Spirit helps us in our weakness; for we do not know how to pray as we ought, but that very Spirit intercedes with sighs too deep for words. And God, who searches the heart, knows what is the mind of the Spirit, because the Spirit intercedes for the saints according to the will of God. We know that all things work together for good for those who love God, who are called according to his purpose.

Reader: We know the Holy Spirit hears our sorrows and inter-cedes on our behalf, and God who loves us gives us comfort. We have experienced God's love in our lives in many ways, but we are also reminded that God's love is reflected by us when we show love to others. It is in the reflection of our love that we live in God and that we know God lives in us. In 1 John 4:11-19 we read:

> *Since God loved us so much, we also ought to love one another. No one has ever seen God; if we love one another, God lives in us, and his love is perfected in us. By this we know that we abide in him and he in us, because he has given us of his Spirit. And we have seen and do testify that the Father has sent his Son as the Savior of the world. God abides in those who con-fess that Jesus is the Son of God, and they abide in God. So we have known and believe the love that God has for us. God is love, and those who abide in love abide in God, and God abides in them. Love has been perfected among us in this: that we may have bold-ness on the day of judgment, because as he is, so are we in this world. There is no fear in love, but perfect love casts out fear; for fear has to do with punish-ment, and whoever fears has not reached perfection in love. We love because he first loved us.*

Meditation and Prayer

Leader: These words calm our fears and offer us comfort and hope. Let us have a moment of silence to contemplate the reassurance we receive through our Lord's love perfected in us. *(Silence)* Let us pray: Heavenly Fa-ther, you have given us life on earth and eternal life because you love us. May we return that love to you and to others who touch our lives. We give you thanks and praise. In Jesus' name. Amen.

Reading from Saint Paul's Letters to the Romans

Reader: We are assured that a new creation awaits us. Yet, as we wait in patience, we see in this world the workings of sin and the fear of death. In Romans, the Apostle Paul answers the question, "How can we who died to sin go on living in it?" He reminds us of God's promise and assures us that all who believe in Christ will win the victory over death and will have joy in the new life that awaits us.

Do you not know that all of us who have been baptized into Christ Jesus were baptized into his death? Therefore we have been buried with him by baptism into death, so that, just as Christ was raised from the dead by the glory of the Father, so we too might walk in newness of life. For if we have been united with him in a death like his, we will certainly be united with him in a resurrection like his. We know that our old self was crucified with him so that the body of sin might be destroyed, and we might no longer be enslaved to sin. For whoever has died is freed from sin. But if we have died with Christ, we believe that we will also live with him. We know that Christ, being raised from the dead, will never die again; death no longer has dominion over him. The death he died, he died to sin, once for all; but the life he lives, he lives to God (Romans 6:3-10).

Meditation

Leader: Truly, we have been freed from sin and have received eternal life through Christ. Yet as we heard, we do not sit back and wait for the great day to come, but we live our lives to the glory of God as we wait. We know that indeed _____ did live a life to God. In the next silent moments, you are asked to consider ways in which _____ touched your life in actions of love, comfort, joy, and friendship. (*Silence*) We ask if there are any thoughts or memories that you would

like to share with us today, special ways in which
_____ touched your life.

A Time for Sharing
(The leader will allow time for recollections.)

Comfort for the Living:
Reader: In Revelation we are assured,

> *See I am making all things new. Write this, for these words are trustworthy and true. It is done! I am the Alpha and the Omega, the beginning and the end. To the thirsty, I will give water as a gift from the spring of the water of life* (Revelation 21:5-6).

We know a new life awaits us all as the Bible assures us:

> *So if anyone is in Christ, there is a new creation, everything old has passed away; see, everything has become new! All this is from God, who reconciled us to himself through Christ, and has given us the ministry of reconciliation* (2 Corinthians 5:17-18).

Leader: We praise you, Lord, for the reconciliation we received through Jesus Christ. Like David of old, we, too, sing your praise.

Responsive Reading from Psalm 96:1-4, 13
Reader: O sing to the Lord a new song; sing to the Lord, all the earth.

Response: **Sing to the Lord, bless his name; tell of his salvation from day to day.**

Reader: Declare his glory among the nations, his marvelous works among all the peoples.

Response: **For great is the Lord, and greatly to be praised; he is to be revered above all gods.**

Reader: For he is coming, for he is coming to judge the earth. He will judge the world with righteousness, and the peoples with his truth.

Response: O sing to the Lord a new song; sing to the Lord, all the earth.

Leader: Let us pray the prayer our Lord taught us to pray:

All: **Our Father which art in heaven, hallowed be thy name. Thy kingdom come. Thy will be done in earth, as it is in heaven. Give us this day our daily bread. And forgive us our debts, as we forgive our debtors. And lead us not into temptation, but deliver us from evil: For thine is the kingdom, and the power, and the glory, for ever. Amen.**

Closing Prayer

Leader: God the Father, Creator of all, we thank you for the promise of a new creation and the gift of life eternal. We thank you, Lord, for the comfort and assurance we receive through your Word, confident that _____ lives today with you in heaven. Be with those who mourn, comforting them with the presence of the Holy Spirit. Guide and protect us all until the day comes when we, too, join our loved ones to live with you forever in your heavenly kingdom. We ask this in Jesus' name. Amen.

(The service is concluded.)

You Are A New Creation

(The participants will read the portions of the service marked as **Response** *and* **All.***)*

Opening Invocation

Responsive Reading from Isaiah 42:5-10
Reader: Thus says God, the Lord, who created the heavens and stretched them out, who spread out the earth and what comes from it, who gives breath to the people upon it and spirit to those who walk in it:
Response: **I am the Lord, I have called you in righteousness, I have taken you by the hand and kept you; I have given you as a covenant to the people, a light to the nations,**
Reader: To open the eyes that are blind, to bring out the prisoners from the dungeon, from the prison those who sit in darkness.
Response: **I am the Lord, that is my name; my glory I give to no other, nor my praise to idols.**
Reader: See, the former things have come to pass, and new things I now declare; before they spring forth, I tell you of them.
Response: **Sing to the Lord a new song, his praise from the end of the earth!**

Prayer

Old Testament Responsive Reading from Psalm 119
Reader: Let your steadfast love come to me, O Lord, your salvation according to your promise.
Response: **Then I shall have an answer for those who taunt me, for I trust in your word.**

Reader:	Your hands have made and fashioned me; give me understanding that I may learn your commandments.
Response:	**Those who fear you shall see me and rejoice, because I have hoped in your word.**
Leader:	I know, O Lord, that your judgments are right, and that in faithfulness you have humbled me.
Response:	**Let your steadfast love become my comfort according to your promise to your servant.**
Leader:	Let your mercy come to me, that I may live; for your law is my delight.
Response:	**Let your steadfast love come to me, O Lord, your salvation according to your promise.**

New Testament Readings

Meditation and Prayer

Reading from Saint Paul's Letters to the Romans

Meditation

A Time for Sharing

Comfort for the Living

Responsive Reading from Psalm 96:1-4, 13

Reader:	O sing to the Lord a new song; sing to the Lord, all the earth.
Response:	**Sing to the Lord, bless his name; tell of his salvation from day to day.**
Reader:	Declare his glory among the nations, his marvelous works among all the peoples.
Response:	**For great is the Lord, and greatly to be praised; he is to be revered above all gods.**
Reader:	For he is coming, for he is coming to judge the earth. He will judge the world with righteousness, and the peoples with his truth.

31

Response: O sing to the Lord a new song; sing to the Lord, all
the earth.

The Lord's Prayer
All: Our Father which art in heaven, hallowed be thy
name. Thy kingdom come. Thy will be done in earth,
as it is in heaven. Give us this day our daily bread.
And forgive us our debts, as we forgive our debtors. And lead us not into temptation, but deliver us
from evil: For thine is the kingdom, and the power,
and the glory, for ever. Amen.

Closing Prayer

Service 3

On Eagles' Wings

(Family and friends are called to silence for the opening of the prayer service.)

Opening Invocation

Leader: In the name of the Father and of the Son and of the Holy Spirit. Amen.

Yours, O Lord, are the greatness, the power, the glory, the victory, and the majesty; for all that is in the heavens and on the earth is yours; yours is the kingdom, O Lord, and you are exalted as head above all. Riches and honor come from you, and you rule over all. In your hand are power and might; and it is in your hand to make great and to give strength to all. And now, our God, we give thanks to you and praise your glorious name (1 Chronicles 29:11-13).

We gather this day to celebrate the victory of _____ who has soared above this world of sin and pain and on eagles' wings was carried to the Father in heaven. We thank you, Lord, for your constant care and protection and especially for giving us your Son, Jesus Christ, who assures us a place in your heavenly kingdom.

Responsive Reading from Isaiah 40:28-31

Reader: Have you not known? Have you not heard? The Lord is the everlasting God, the Creator of the ends of the earth. He does not faint or grow weary; his understanding is unsearchable.

Response: **He gives power to the faint, and strengthens the powerless.**

Reader: Even youths will faint and be weary, and the young will fall exhausted;

Response: **But those who wait for the Lord shall renew their strength, they shall mount up with wings like eagles, they shall run and not be weary, they shall walk and not faint.**

Prayer

Leader: Let us pray. Heavenly Father, you are powerful and mighty. You lift us up on the wings of eagles and carry us in your protective arms. Your majesty is revealed to us daily as we view your creation. We thank you for our lives, gifts from you, and we praise you for the life which you have prepared for us in heaven. Comfort those who mourn this day with the knowledge that one day we will all rise on eagles' wings to live with you in heaven and meet again those we love who have gone on before us. In Jesus' name we pray. Amen

Old Testament Responsive Reading

Leader: As an eagle stirs up its nest, and hovers over its young; as it spreads its wings, takes them up, and bears them aloft on its pinion (Deuteronomy 32:11), so the Lord watches over his children. We read in Psalm 103:1-18:

Reader: Bless the Lord, O my soul, and all that is within me, bless his holy name.

Response: **Bless the Lord, O my soul, and do not forget all his benefits —**

Reader: Who forgives all your iniquity, who heals all your diseases,

Response: **Who redeems your life from the Pit, who crowns you with steadfast love and mercy,**

Reader: Who satisfies you with good as long as you live so that your youth is renewed like the eagle's.

Response: **The Lord works vindication and justice for all who are oppressed.**

Reader: He made known his ways to Moses, his acts to the people of Israel.

Response: The Lord is merciful and gracious, slow to anger and abounding in steadfast love.

Reader: He will not always accuse, nor will he keep his anger forever.

Response: He does not deal with us according to our sins, nor repay us according to our iniquities.

Reader: For as the heavens are high above the earth, so great is his steadfast love toward those who fear him;

Response: As far as the east is from the west, so far he removes our transgressions from us.

Reader: As a father has compassion for his children, so the Lord has compassion for those who fear him.

Response: For he knows how we were made; he remembers that we are dust.

Reader: As for mortals, their days are like grass; they flourish like a flower of the field;

Response: For the wind passes over it, and it is gone, and its place knows it no more.

Reader: But the steadfast love of the Lord is from everlasting to everlasting on those who fear him, and his righteousness to children's children,

Response: To those who keep his covenant and remember to do his commandments. Bless the Lord, O my soul, and all that is within me, bless his holy name.

New Testament Readings

Leader: God's love endures forever and gives us strength. We are reminded in Colossians 1:11-20:

May you be made strong with all the strength that comes from his glorious power, and may you be prepared to endure everything with patience, while joyfully giving thanks to the Father, who has enabled you to share in the inheritance of the saints in the light. He has rescued us from the power of darkness and transferred us into the kingdom of his beloved Son, in whom

35

we have redemption, the forgiveness of sins. He is the image of the invisible God, the firstborn of all creation; for in him all things in heaven and on earth were created, things visible and invisible, whether thrones or dominions or rulers or powers — all things have been created through him and for him. He himself is before all things, and in him all things hold together. He is the head of the body, the church; he is the beginning, the firstborn from the dead, so that he might come to have first place in everything. For in him all the fullness of God was pleased to dwell, and through him God was pleased to reconcile to himself all things, whether on earth or in heaven, by making peace through the blood of his cross.

Responsive Reading

Leader: We are heirs to the kingdom through the death and resurrection of our Lord, Jesus Christ. In John 6:35-40, Jesus reminds us,

Reader: "I am the bread of life. Whoever comes to me will never be hungry, and whoever believes in me will never be thirsty.

Response: **But I said to you that you have seen me and yet do not believe.**

Reader: Everything that the Father gives me will come to me, and anyone who comes to me I will never drive away;

Response: **For I have come down from heaven, not to do my own will, but the will of him who sent me.**

Reader: And this is the will of him who sent me, that I should lose nothing of all that he has given me, but raise it up on the last day.

Response: **This is indeed the will of my Father, that all who see the Son and believe in him may have eternal life; and I will raise them up on the last day."**

Meditation and Prayer

Leader: Our Lord, Jesus Christ, has promised to be with us in life and in death, if we believe in him, true Son of the Father, born sinless into a sinful world, so that his death would give us life. We will share a moment of silence as we remember Jesus' words, "I am the bread of life. Whoever comes to me will never be hungry, and whoever believes in me will never be thirsty." (*Silence*) Let us pray: God, our Father, you gave us your Son as a willing sacrifice for our sin. You give us bread for our bodies and Jesus, the Bread of Life, for our souls. We give you thanks and praise for the gifts you give us freely and in steadfast love. In Jesus' name. Amen.

Reading from Isaiah 46:3-11

Reader: God assures us that we are his even from before our birth and to our death. God also promises us salvation, planned before man's fall in the Garden of Eden. We read in Isaiah:

Listen to me, O house of Jacob, all the remnant of the house of Israel, who have been borne by me from your birth, carried from the womb; even to your old age I am he, even when you turn gray I will carry you. I have made, and I will bear; I will carry and will save. To whom will you liken me and make me equal, and compare me, as though we were alike? Those who lavish gold from the purse, and weigh out silver in the scales — they hire a goldsmith, who makes it into a god; then they fall down and worship! They lift it to their shoulders, they carry it, they set it in its place, and it stands there; it cannot move from its place. If one cries out to it, it does not answer or save anyone from trouble. Remember this and consider, recall it to mind, you transgressors, remember the former things of old; for I am God, and there is no other; I am God, and there is no one like me, declaring the end from the

beginning and from ancient times things not yet done,
saying, "My purpose shall stand, and I will fulfill my
intention," calling a bird of prey from the east, the man
for my purpose from a far country. I have spoken, and
I will bring it to pass; I have planned, and I will do it.

Meditation

Leader: God's promise of salvation gives us comfort and hope.
In Matthew 4:4, we are reminded: "It is written, One
does not live by bread alone, but by every word that
comes from the mouth of God." God gave us his Son,
our bread of life, who offers us eternal life, but we in
turn can offer something back to the world. The Bible
teaches us to love, comfort, and give guidance and
compassion to all who are in need. Let us remember
the times when _____ provided us with
love, comfort, guidance, and compassion, touching our
lives in unique ways. We will take a few moments of
silence to think about these special experiences which
we shared with _____. (*Silence*) We ask you
now if there are any thoughts or memories which you
would like to share with us today.

A Time for Sharing

(*The leader will allow time for recollections.*)

Comfort for the Living:

Reader: *And Jesus said, "Come to me, all you that are weary*
and are carrying heavy burdens, and I will give you
rest. Take my yoke upon you, and learn from me; for I
am gentle and humble in heart, and you will find rest
for your souls. For my yoke is easy, and my burden is
light" (Matthew 11:28-30).

Leader: You have heard Jesus' words, "Come to me." Do not
bear your sorrow alone. Our Lord, Jesus Christ, is willing to bear your burdens with you. The Comforter, the

Holy Spirit, can raise you above pain and grief of this world. God reminds us,

I bore you on eagles' wings and brought you to myself. Now therefore, if you obey my voice and keep my covenant, you shall be my treasured possession out of all the peoples (Exodus 19:4-5).

Responsory Reading from Psalm 28:6-9

Reader: Let us give thanks to God. Blessed be the Lord, for he has heard the sound of my pleadings.

Response: The Lord is my strength and my shield; in him my heart trusts; so I am helped, and my heart exults, and with my song I give thanks to him.

Reader: The Lord is the strength of his people; he is the saving refuge of his anointed.

Response: O save your people, and bless your heritage; be their shepherd, and carry them forever.

Leader: Let us pray the prayer our Lord taught us to pray:

All: Our Father which art in heaven, hallowed be thy name. Thy kingdom come. Thy will be done in earth, as it is in heaven. Give us this day our daily bread. And forgive us our debts, as we forgive our debtors. And lead us not into temptation, but deliver us from evil: For thine is the kingdom, and the power, and the glory, for ever. Amen.

Closing Prayer

Leader: *Yours, O Lord, are the greatness, the power, the glory, the victory, and the majesty; for all that is in the heavens and on the earth is yours; yours is the kingdom, O Lord, and you are exalted as head above all. Riches and honor come from you, and you rule over all. In your hands are power and might; and it is in your hand to make great and to give strength to all. And now, our God, we give thanks to you and praise your glorious name* (1 Chronicles 29:11-13).

We thank you for offering us hope of life eternal. Father, we ask you to comfort those who mourn. Renew us with your Word, as we wait for the day we join those we love in heaven. Raise us up on eagles' wings and hold us in the palm of your hand. In the name of our Lord, Jesus Christ. Amen.

(The service is concluded.)

On Eagles' Wings

(The participants will read the portions of the service marked **Response** *and* **All.***)*

Opening Invocation

Responsive Reading from Isaiah 40:28-31

Reader: Have you not known? Have you not heard? The Lord is the everlasting God, the Creator of the ends of the earth. He does not faint or grow weary; his understanding is unsearchable.

Response: **He gives power to the faint, and strengthens the powerless.**

Reader: Even youths will faint and be weary, and the young will fall exhausted;

Response: **But those who wait for the Lord shall renew their strength, they shall mount up with wings like eagles, they shall run and not be weary, they shall walk and not faint.**

Prayer

Old Testament Responsive Reading from Psalm 103:1-18

Reader: Bless the Lord, O my soul, and all that is within me, bless his holy name.

Response: **Bless the Lord, O my soul, and do not forget all his benefits —**

Reader: Who forgives all your iniquity, who heals all your diseases,

Response: **Who redeems your life from the Pit, who crowns you with steadfast love and mercy,**

Reader: Who satisfies you with good as long as you live so that your youth is renewed like the eagle's.

41

Response: **The Lord works vindication and justice for all who are oppressed.**

Reader: He made known his ways to Moses, his acts to the people of Israel.

Response: **The Lord is merciful and gracious, slow to anger and abounding in steadfast love.**

Reader: He will not always accuse, nor will he keep his anger forever.

Response: **He does not deal with us according to our sins, nor repay us according to our iniquities.**

Reader: For as the heavens are high above the earth, so great is his steadfast love toward those who fear him;

Response: **As far as the east is from the west, so far he removes our transgressions from us.**

Reader: As a father has compassion for his children, so the Lord has compassion for those who fear him.

Response: **For he knows how we were made; he remembers that we are dust.**

Reader: As for mortals, their days are like grass; they flourish like a flower of the field;

Response: **For the wind passes over it, and it is gone, and its place knows it no more.**

Reader: But the steadfast love of the Lord is from everlasting to everlasting on those who fear him, and his righteousness to children's children,

Response: **To those who keep his covenant and remember to do his commandments. Bless the Lord, O my soul, and all that is within me, bless his holy name.**

New Testament Reading

Responsive Reading from John 6:35-40

Reader: Jesus said to them, "I am the bread of life. Whoever comes to me will never be hungry, and whoever believes in me will never be thirsty.

Response: **But I said to you that you have seen me and yet do not believe.**

Reader: Everything that the Father gives me will come to me, and anyone who comes to me I will never drive away;

Response: For I have come down from heaven, not to do my own will, but the will of him who sent me.

Reader: And this is the will of him who sent me, that I should lose nothing of all that he has given me, but raise it up on the last day.

Response: This is indeed the will of my Father, that all who see the Son and believe in him may have eternal life; and I will raise them up on the last day."

Meditation and Prayer

Reading from Isaiah 46:3-11

Meditation

A Time for Sharing

Comfort for the Living

Responsive Reading from Psalm 28:6-9

Reader: Let us give thanks to God. Blessed be the Lord, for he has heard the sound of my pleadings.

Response: The Lord is my strength and my shield; in him my heart trusts; so I am helped, and my heart exults, and with my song I give thanks to him.

Reader: The Lord is the strength of his people; he is the saving refuge of his anointed.

Response: O save your people, and bless your heritage; be their shepherd, and carry them forever.

The Lord's Prayer

All: Our Father which art in heaven, hallowed be thy name. Thy kingdom come. Thy will be done in earth, as it is in heaven. Give us this day our daily bread.

43

And forgive us our debts, as we forgive our debtors. And lead us not into temptation, but deliver us from evil: For thine is the kingdom, and the power, and the glory, for ever. Amen.

Closing Prayer

Service 4

The Gift Of Life

(Family and friends are called to silence for the opening of the prayer service.)

Opening Invocation

Leader: In the name of the Father and of the Son and of the Holy Spirit. Amen. "For the wages of sin is death, but the free gift of God is eternal life in Christ Jesus our Lord" (Romans 6:23). We gather today to celebrate the life of _____ who has been given life anew through God's miraculous gift of his Son. All life is a gift from God our creator. In Nehemiah 9:6, we read,
You alone are the Lord, you have made heaven, the heaven of heavens, with all their hosts, the earth, and all that is on it, the seas and all that is in them. To all of them you give life, and the host of heaven worships you. We give God thanks and praise for the gift of eternal life for all who believe in his Son, Jesus Christ who was born to be the Savior of the world.

Responsive Reading from John 10:27-30

Reader: My sheep hear my voice.
Response: I know them, and they follow me.
Reader: I give them eternal life, and they will never perish.
Response: No one will snatch them out of my hand.
Reader: What my Father has given me is greater than all else,
Response: And no one can snatch it out of the Father's hand. The Father and I are one.

Prayer

Leader: Let us pray. Father Creator, you have given us life, a gift from your bountiful hand. Knowing our sinful nature, you planned for our salvation by giving us your

45

Son, who in turn gave his life for us on the cross. We give you thanks and praise. Give comfort to those who grieve with the assurance that eternal life waits for all who believer. In Jesus' name we pray. Amen.

Old Testament Responsive Reading from Psalm 119:151-156, 165-166

Reader: Yet you are near, O Lord, and all your commandments are true.

Response: Long ago I learned from your decrees that you have established them forever.

Reader: Look on my misery and rescue me, for I do not forget your law.

Response: Plead my cause and redeem me; give me life according to your promise.

Reader: Salvation is far from the wicked, for they do not seek your statutes.

Response: Great is your mercy, O Lord; give me life according to your justice.

Reader: Great peace have those who love your law; nothing can make them stumble.

Response: I hope for your salvation, O Lord, and I fulfill your commandments.

New Testament Readings

Leader: The Bible guarantees salvation for those who live according to God's commands, not clinging to things of this earth, but clinging to the love of the Lord and the belief in Jesus Christ as our Savior. Romans 8:9-11 tells us:

But you are not in the flesh; you are in the Spirit, since the Spirit of God dwells in you. Anyone who does not have the Spirit of Christ does not belong to him. But if Christ is in you, though the body is dead because of sin, the Spirit is life because of righteousness. If the Spirit of him who raised Jesus from the dead dwells in you, he who raised Christ from the dead

46

will give life to your mortal bodies also through his Spirit that dwells in you.

On the night before Jesus died, he knelt in the Garden of Gethsemane and prayed to his Father. The prayer assures us that God's plan was complete. We read in John 17:1-8:

After Jesus had spoken these words, he looked up to heaven and said, "Father, the hour has come; glorify your Son so that the Son may glorify you, since you have given him authority over all people, to give eternal life to all whom you have given him. And this is eternal life, that they may know you, the only true God, and Jesus Christ whom you have sent. I glorified you on earth by finishing the work that you gave me to do. So now, Father, glorify me in your own presence with the glory that I had in your presence before the world existed. I have made your name known to those whom you gave me from the world. They were yours, and you gave them to me, and they have kept your word. Now they know that everything you have given me is from you; for the words that you gave to me I have given to them, and they have received them and know in truth that I came from you; and they have believed that you sent me."

Responsive Reading:

Leader: God, the Father, sent his Son to die for our sins and give us an eternal home in heaven. Like bread which nourishes our bodies, Jesus tells us that he is the bread which comes from heaven to nourish our souls. In John 6:51-58, he says:

Reader: I am the living bread that came down from heaven.

Response: Whoever eats of this bread will live forever;

Reader: And the bread that I will give for the life of the world is my flesh.

Response: The Jews then disputed among themselves, saying, "How can this man give us his flesh to eat?"

Reader:	So Jesus said to them, "Very truly, I tell you, unless you eat the flesh of the Son of Man and drink his blood, you have no life in you.
Response:	**Those who eat my flesh and drink my blood have eternal life,**
Reader:	And I will raise them up on the last day; for my flesh is true food and my blood is true drink.
Response:	**Those who eat my flesh and drink my blood abide in me, and I in them.**
Reader:	Just as the living Father sent me, and I live because of the Father,
Response:	**So whoever eats me will live because of me.**
Reader:	This is the bread that came down from heaven, not like that which your ancestors ate, and they died.
Response:	**But the one who eats this bread will live forever."**

Meditation and Prayer

Leader: Jesus Christ, our Redeemer, is our Bread from Heaven, a gift from the Father to a world of sinful men, so that we might be saved. In silence, let us reflect upon the these words:

For the Son of Man came not to be served but to serve, and to give his life a ransom for many (Mark 10:45).

(*Silence*) Let us pray. Father, Creator, we give you thanks for the wonders you have given us, the earth, the sky, and our own being. We belong to you, and therefore, we must remember you can call us at your will to be with you in our home in heaven. Help us to understand that we are here only a little while. We are with you in heaven for eternity. In the name of Jesus, our Gift of Life. Amen.

Reading from Matthew 16:24-27

Reader: We see that our lives are gifts. How should we live the life that the Father has given us? How does the Lord expect us to behave? In Matthew 16, we read:

48

Then Jesus told his disciples, "If any want to become my followers, let them deny themselves and take up their cross and follow me. For those who want to save their life will lose it, and those who lose their life for my sake will find it. For what will it profit them if they gain the whole world but forfeit their life? Or what will they give in return for their life? For the Son of Man is to come with his angels in the glory of his Father, and then he will repay everyone for what has been done."

Meditation

Leader: As was heard, we are to take up the cross and follow Jesus, doing the will of the Father. In Romans 2:6 we read:

For [God] will repay according to each one's deeds: to those who by patiently doing good seek for glory and honor and immortality, he will give eternal life.

This message reminds us that our lives are not measured by the material things we accumulate, but by the way in which we have touched lives according to God's commandments. _____ has touched our lives in many ways. Let us take a few silent moments to think about the special ways _____ has affected our lives. (*Silence*) Now we ask if family and friends would like to share with us any special ways in which _____ touched their lives.

A Time for Sharing

(*The leader will allow time for recollections.*)

Comfort for the Living

Reader: *Jesus said, "Very truly, I tell you, the Son can do nothing on his own, but only what he sees the Father doing; for whatever the Father does, the Son does likewise. The Father loves the Son and shows him all that*

49

he himself is doing; and he will show him greater works than these, so that you will be astonished. Indeed, just as the Father raises the dead and gives them life, so also the Son gives life to whomever he wishes. The Father judges no one but has given all judgment to the Son, so that all may honor the Son just as they honor the Father. Anyone who does not honor the Son does not honor the Father who sent him. Very truly, I tell you, anyone who hears my word and believes him who sent me has eternal life, and does not come under judgment, but has passed from death to life" (John 5:19-24).

Leader: You have heard Jesus' words, "Very truly, I tell you, anyone who hears my word and believes him who sent me has eternal life." You are assured that today _____ and all who have died in the Lord live together in heaven. We praise you, God, for your mercy and comfort which comes to us from the Holy Spirit.

Responsive Reading from Psalm 119:35-41

Reader: Lead me in the path of your commandments, for I delight in it.

Response: **Turn my heart to your decrees, and not to selfish gain.**

Reader: Turn my eyes from looking at vanities; give me life in your ways.

Response: **Confirm to your servant your promise, which is for those who fear you.**

Reader: Turn away the disgrace that I dread, for your ordinances are good.

Response: **See, I have longed for your precepts; in your righteousness give me life.**

All: **Let your steadfast love come to me, O Lord, your salvation according to your promise.**

Leader: Let us pray the prayer our Lord taught us:

50

All: **Our Father which art in heaven, hallowed be thy name. Thy kingdom come. Thy will be done in earth, as it is in heaven. Give us this day our daily bread. And forgive us our debts, as we forgive our debtors. And lead us not into temptation, but deliver us from evil: For thine is the kingdom, and the power, and the glory, for ever. Amen.**

Closing Prayer

Leader: *Then he said to me, "It is done! I am the Alpha and the Omega, the beginning and the end. To the thirsty I will give water as a gift from the spring of the water of life. Those who conquer will inherit these things, and I will be their God and they will be my children"* (Revelation 21:6-7).

We thank you Heavenly Father for the cooling waters which you offer us from the heavenly springs. You guide us and keep us safe through all our days, and when our time has come, you carry us to your home in heaven. Comfort us with your steadfast love and guide our footsteps until our gift is complete, the gift of life eternal. In Jesus' name we pray. Amen.

(The service is concluded.)

The Gift Of Life

(The participants will read the portions of the service marked **Response** *and* **All.***)*

Opening Invocation

Responsive Reading from John 10:27-30
Reader: My sheep hear my voice.
Response: **I know them, and they follow me.**
Reader: I give them eternal life, and they will never perish.
Response: **No one will snatch them out of my hand.**
Reader: What my Father has given me is greater than all else,
Response: **And no one can snatch it out of the Father's hand. The Father and I are one.**

Prayer

Old Testament Responsive Reading from Psalm 119:151-156, 165-166
Reader: Yet you are near, O Lord, and all your commandments are true.
Response: **Long ago I learned from your decrees that you have established them forever.**
Reader: Look on my misery and rescue me, for I do not forget your law.
Response: **Plead my cause and redeem me; give me life according to your promise.**
Reader: Salvation is far from the wicked, for they do not seek your statutes.
Response: **Great is your mercy, O Lord; give me life according to your justice.**
Reader: Great peace have those who love your law; nothing can make them stumble.

Response: I hope for your salvation, O Lord, and I fulfill your commandments.

New Testament Readings

Responsive Reading from John 6:51-58

Reader: I am the living bread that came down from heaven.

Response: Whoever eats of this bread will live forever;

Reader: And the bread that I will give for the life of the world is my flesh.

Response: The Jews then disputed among themselves, saying, "How can this man give us his flesh to eat?"

Reader: So Jesus said to them, "Very truly, I tell you, unless you eat the flesh of the Son of Man and drink his blood, you have no life in you.

Response: Those who eat my flesh and drink my blood have eternal life,

Reader: And I will raise them up on the last day; for my flesh is true food and my blood is true drink.

Response: Those who eat my flesh and drink my blood abide in me, and I in them.

Reader: Just as the living Father sent me, and I live because of the Father,

Response: So whoever eats me will live because of me.

Reader: This is the bread that came down from heaven, not like that which your ancestors ate, and they died.

Response: But the one who eats this bread will live forever."

Meditation and Prayer

Reading from Matthew 16:24-27

Meditation

A Time for Sharing

Comfort for the Living

53

Responsive Reading from Psalm 119:35-41

Reader: Lead me in the path of your commandments, for I delight in it.

Response: **Turn my heart to your decrees, and not to selfish gain.**

Reader: Turn my eyes from looking at vanities; give me life in your ways.

Response: **Confirm to your servant your promise, which is for those who fear you.**

Reader: Turn away the disgrace that I dread, for your ordinances are good.

Response: **See, I have longed for your precepts; in your righteousness give me life.**

All: **Let your steadfast love come to me, O Lord, your salvation according to your promise.**

The Lord's Prayer

All: **Our Father which art in heaven, hallowed be thy name. Thy kingdom come. Thy will be done in earth, as it is in heaven. Give us this day our daily bread. And forgive us our debts, as we forgive our debtors. And lead us not into temptation, but deliver us from evil: For thine is the kingdom, and the power, and the glory, for ever. Amen.**

Closing Prayer

Service 5

I Am The Resurrection

(Family and friends are called to silence for the opening of the prayer service.)

Opening Invocation
Leader: We begin in the name of the Father and of the Son and of the Holy Spirit. Amen.

Blessed be the God and Father of our Lord Jesus Christ! By his great mercy he has given us a new birth into a living hope through the resurrection of Jesus Christ from the dead, and into an inheritance that is imperishable, undefiled, and unfading, kept in heaven for you, who are being protected by the power of God through faith for a salvation ready to be revealed in the last time (1 Peter 1:3-5).

Today we celebrate the death and new life of _____ who was taken home to heaven. God has given us the promise of salvation and the comfort of the Holy Spirit. Through the resurrection of our Lord, Jesus Christ, we, too, will rise to live with God and all those we love in heaven.

Responsive Reading from Psalm 17:5-8; 18:1-3
Reader: My steps have held fast to your paths;
Response: **My feet have not slipped.**
Reader: I call upon you, for you will answer me, O God;
Response: **Incline your ear to me, hear my words.**
Reader: Wondrously show your steadfast love, O savior of those who seek refuge from their adversaries at your right hand.
Response: **Guard me as the apple of the eye;**
Reader: Hide me in the shadow of your wings,
Response: **I love you, O Lord, my strength.**

55

Reader: The Lord is my rock, my fortress, and my deliverer, my God, my rock in whom I take refuge, my shield, and the horn of my salvation, my stronghold.

Response: I call upon the Lord, who is worthy to be praised.

Prayer

Leader: Let us pray. Heavenly Father, our rock and fortress, you have given us the greatest gift of all, your Son, Jesus Christ, whose death gives us life. We thank and praise your for your loving care. Open our hearts to your Word and the hope and comfort we have in our salvation. Amen.

Old Testament Responsive Reading

Leader: We find comfort in God's word. In steadfast love, God's promise gives us life. We read in Psalm 119 selected verses:

Reader: Remember your word to your servant, in which you have made me hope.

Response: This is my comfort in my distress, that your promise gives me life.

Reader: The earth, O Lord, is full of your steadfast love; teach me your statutes.

Response: You have dealt well with your servant, O Lord, according to your word.

Reader: Your hands have made and fashioned me; give me understanding that I may learn your commandments.

Response: Those who fear you shall see me and rejoice, because I have hoped in your word.

Reader: I know, O Lord, that your judgments are right, and that in faithfulness you have humbled me.

Response: Let your steadfast love become my comfort according to your promise to your servant.

New Testament Readings

Leader: God's plan for our salvation was revealed to us in the Garden of Eden, when God said to Adam and Eve in

Genesis 3:15, "I will put enmity between you and the woman, and between your offspring and hers; he will strike your head, and you will strike his heel." In their humanity, Adam and Eve sinned, bringing to the world human death, but God promised us his Son, Jesus Christ, who by his death and resurrection brings us eternal life. Listen to the message in 1 Corinthians:

But in fact Christ has been raised from the dead, the first fruits of those who have died. For since death came through a human being, the resurrection of the dead has also come through a human being; for as all die in Adam, so all will be made alive in Christ. But each in his own order: Christ the first fruits, then at his coming those who belong to Christ. Then comes the end, when he hands over the kingdom to God the Father, after he has destroyed every ruler and every authority and power. For he must reign until he has put all his enemies under his feet. The last enemy to be destroyed is death (1 Corinthians 15:20-26).

So it is with the resurrection of the dead. What is sown is perishable, what is raised is imperishable. It is sown in dishonor, it is raised in glory. It is sown in weakness, it is raised in power. It is sown a physical body, it is raised a spiritual body. If there is a physical body, there is also a spiritual body. Thus it is written, "The first man, Adam, became a living being"; the last Adam became a life-giving spirit. But it is not the spiritual that is first, but the physical, and then the spiritual. The first man was from the earth, a man of dust; the second man is from heaven. As was the man of dust, so are those who are of the dust; and as is the man of heaven, so are those who are of heaven. Just as we have borne the image of the man of dust, we will also bear the image of the man of heaven (1 Corinthians 15:42-49).

Meditation and Prayer

Leader: Our resurrection is assured as we recall the words, "For as all die in Adam, so all will be made alive in Christ." In silence, let us meditate on these Words of God. (*Silence*) Let us pray. Lord, you have cared for us before the earth was made. In the Garden of Eden, you gave us the greatest of gifts forgiveness of sin and eternal life. You have said, "What is sown is perishable, what is raised is imperishable." We give you thanks and praise. In the name of the Resurrected Christ. Amen.

Reading from the Gospel of John

Reader: Jesus received a message from the sisters of Lazarus, one of Jesus' best friends, telling Jesus that Lazarus was near death. Jesus went to Bethany, knowing that Lazarus had died and lay four days in the tomb. Jesus said to the disciples, "For your sake I am glad I was not there, so that you may believe." Lazarus' death and resurrection was to explain and mirror to the world the resurrection of Christ. We read in John 11:17-26:

When Jesus arrived, he found that Lazarus had already been in the tomb four days. Now Bethany was near Jerusalem, some two miles away, and many of the Jews had come to Martha and Mary to console them about their brother. When Martha heard that Jesus was coming, she went and met him, while Mary stayed at home. Martha said to Jesus, "Lord, if you had been here, my brother would not have died. But even now I know that God will give you whatever you ask of him." Jesus said to her, "Your brother will rise again." Martha said to him, "I know that he will rise again in the resurrection on the last day." Jesus said to her, "I am the resurrection and the life. Those who believe in me, even though they die, will live, and everyone who lives and believes in me will never die."

58

Meditation

Leader: Friends of Mary and Martha gathered together in Bethany to offer consolation to them in their grief. Today family and friends gather here to give consolation to one another, as we ponder the loss of _____. Our support for one another, in part, is the sharing of memories, recalling the way _____ touched our lives. Let us recall those memories during this moment of silence. (*Silence*) In your recollections, you may have special memories that you would like to share at this time, ways in which _____ touched your life.

A Time for Sharing
(*The leader will allow time for recollections.*)

Comfort for the Living

Reader: Even in our sorrow, we remember that as Jesus was present to raise his friend Lazarus from the dead, so he has raised _____ to the newness of life in heaven. The story of Lazarus is to serve as an assurance for us that we and all believers will be raised up to live again. At the raising of Lazarus, Jesus said,
"Did I not tell you that if you believed, you would see the glory of God?" And Jesus looked upward and said, "Father, I thank you for having heard me. I knew that you always hear me, but I have said this for the sake of the crowd standing here, so that they may believe that you sent me." When he had said this, he cried with a loud voice, "Lazarus, come out!" The dead man came out, his hands and feet bound with strips of cloth, and his face wrapped in a cloth. Jesus said to them, "Unbind him, and let him go." Many of the Jews therefore, who had come with Mary and had seen what Jesus did, believed in him (John 11:40-45).

Reading from Romans 8:10-11, 13-17

Leader: In the raising of Lazarus, Jesus' message unbinds us from the fear of death and offers us the reassurance of salvation. This does not mean we will feel no pain or sorrow. Listen to the words in Romans 8 beginning with the tenth verse:

But if Christ is in you, though the body is dead because of sin, the Spirit is life because of righteousness. If the Spirit of him who raised Jesus from the dead dwells in you, he who raised Christ from the dead will give life to your mortal bodies also through his Spirit that dwells in you. For if you live according to the flesh, you will die; but if by the Spirit you put to death the deeds of the body, you will live. For all who are led by the Spirit of God are children of God. For you did not receive a spirit of slavery to fall back into fear, but you have received a spirit of adoption. When we cry, "Abba! Father!" it is that very Spirit bearing witness with our spirit that we are children of God, and if children, then heirs, heirs of God and joint heirs with Christ — if, in fact, we suffer with him so that we may also be glorified with him.

Responsive Reading

Leader: As children of God, we are heirs of the kingdom. As Christ suffered and rose from the dead, we, too, will suffer and rise from the dead. The promise in the Garden of Eden has been fulfilled. Death is conquered for us. We read in 1 Corinthians 15:54-57:

Reader: When this perishable body puts on imperishability, and this mortal body puts on immortality,

Response: Then the saying that is written will be fulfilled: "Death has been swallowed up in victory."

Reader: "Where, O death, is your victory?"

Response: "Where, O death, is your sting?"

Reader: The sting of death is sin, and the power of sin is the law.

Response: **But thanks be to God, who gives us the victory through our Lord Jesus Christ.**

Leader: Let us pray the prayer that Jesus taught us to pray:

All: **Our Father which art in heaven, hallowed be thy name. Thy kingdom come. Thy will be done in earth, as it is in heaven. Give us this day our daily bread. And forgive us our debts, as we forgive our debtors. And lead us not into temptation, but deliver us from evil: For thine is the kingdom, and the power, and the glory, forever. Amen.**

Closing Prayer

Leader: Abba Father, you have assured us of our salvation and resurrection. We can boldly say, "Death has been swallowed up in victory." Today, we gather in celebratation, for _____ has obtained victory over death. We ask you to keep us all in your grace. Grant comfort to those who mourn. Your words ring in our ears, "Be faithful until death, and I will give you the crown of life" (Revelation 2:10). We await that day, when we, too, are raised up to live with you and our loved ones in your heavenly kingdom. Jesus said, "I am the resurrection and the life." We thank you for those words of hope and comfort. In Jesus' name we pray. Amen.

(The service is concluded.)

I Am The Resurrection

*(The participants will read the portions of the service marked **Response** and **All**.)*

Opening Invocation

Responsive Reading from Psalm 17:5-8, 18:1-2
Reader: My steps have held fast to your paths;
Response: My feet have not slipped.
Reader: I call upon you, for you will answer me, O God;
Response: Incline your ear to me, hear my words.
Reader: Wondrously show your steadfast love, O savior of those who seek refuge from their adversaries at your right hand.
Response: Guard me as the apple of the eye;
Reader: Hide me in the shadow of your wings,
Response: I love you, O Lord, my strength.
Reader: The Lord is my rock, my fortress, and my deliverer, my God, my rock in whom I take refuge, my shield, and the horn of my salvation, my stronghold.
Response: I call upon the Lord, who is worthy to be praised.

Prayer

Old Testament Responsive Reading from Psalm 119, selected verses
Reader: Remember your word to your servant, in which you have made me hope.
Response: This is my comfort in my distress, that your promise gives me life.
Reader: The earth, O Lord, is full of your steadfast love; teach me your statutes.

Response: You have dealt well with your servant, O Lord, according to your word.

Reader: Your hands have made and fashioned me; give me understanding that I may learn your commandments.

Response: Those who fear you shall see me and rejoice, because I have hoped in your word.

Reader: I know, O Lord, that your judgments are right, and that in faithfulness you have humbled me.

Response: Let your steadfast love become my comfort according to your promise to your servant.

New Testament Readings

Meditation and Prayer

Reading from the Gospel of John

Meditation

A Time for Sharing

Comfort for the Living

Reading from Romans

Responsive Reading from 1 Corinthians 15:54-57

Reader: When this perishable body puts on imperishability, and this mortal body puts on immortality,

Response: Then the saying that is written will be fulfilled: "Death has been swallowed up in victory."

Reader: "Where, O death, is your victory?"

Response: "Where, O death, is your sting?"

Reader: The sting of death is sin, and the power of sin is the law.

Response: But thanks be to God, who gives us the victory through our Lord Jesus Christ.

The Lord's Prayer
All: Our Father which art in heaven, hallowed be thy
              name. Thy kingdom come. Thy will be done in earth,
              as it is in heaven. Give us this day our daily bread.
              And forgive us our debts, as we forgive our debt-
              ors. And lead us not into temptation, but deliver us
              from evil: For thine is the kingdom, and the power,
              and the glory, forever. Amen.

Closing Prayer

Service 6

In My Father's House

(Family and friends are called to silence for the opening of the prayer service.)

Opening Invocation

Leader: We begin in the name of the Father and of the Son and of the Holy Spirit. Amen.

    Do not let your hearts be troubled. Believe in God, believe also in me. In my Father's house there are many dwelling places. If it were not so, would I have told you that I go to prepare a place for you? And if I go and prepare a place for you, I will come again and will take you to myself, so that where I am, there you may be also. And you know the way to the place where I am going. Thomas said to him, "Lord, we do not know where you are going. How can we know the way?" Jesus said to him, "I am the way, and the truth, and the life. No one comes to the Father except through me. If you know me, you will know my Father also. From now on you do know him and have seen him" (John 14:1-7).

    Jesus tells us he has prepared a home in heaven for all believers. We have come here today to celebrate the heavenly homecoming of _____ who has gone to live with God. Through the steadfast love of the heavenly Father, we all await that day when we, too, will join _____ in our heavenly home.

Responsive Reading from Psalms 145, selected verses

Reader: I will extol you, my God and King, and bless your name forever and ever.

Response: **Every day I will bless you, and praise your name forever and ever.**

65

Reader:	Great is the Lord, and greatly to be praised; his greatness is unsearchable.
Response:	**One generation shall laud your works to another, and shall declare your mighty acts.**
Reader:	They shall celebrate the fame of your abundant goodness, and shall sing aloud of your righteousness.
Response:	**The Lord is gracious and merciful, slow to anger and abounding in steadfast love.**
Reader:	The Lord is good to all, and his compassion is over all that he has made.
Response:	**They shall speak of the glory of your kingdom, and tell of your power,**
Reader:	Your kingdom is an everlasting kingdom, and your dominion endures throughout all generations.
Response:	**The Lord is faithful in all his words, and gracious in all his deeds.**
Reader:	The Lord upholds all who are falling, and raises up all who are bowed down.
Response:	**The eyes of all look to you, and you give them their food in due season.**
Reader:	The Lord is near to all who call on him, to all who call on him in truth.
Response:	**The Lord watches over all who love him, but all the wicked he will destroy.**
All:	**My mouth will speak the praise of the Lord, and all flesh will bless his holy name forever and ever.**

Prayer

Leader:	Let us pray. Father in heaven, you hear our prayer and watch over us with your steadfast love. We thank you for your everlasting care. Watch over all who are here today. Open our hearts to your word of hope and comfort. We pray in the name of Jesus. Amen.

Old Testament Responsive Reading

Reader:	The Old Testament speaks to us about God's promise, the promise of Jesus, our Savior, and God's everlasting

love and faithfulness. We read in Psalm 18:30-32, 35, 46:

Reader: This God — his way is perfect; the promise of the Lord proves true; he is a shield for all who take refuge in him.

Response: For who is God except the Lord?

Reader: And who is a rock besides our God? — the God who girded me with strength, and made my way safe.

Response: You have given me the shield of your salvation, and your right hand has supported me; your help has made me great.

All: The Lord lives! Blessed be my rock, and exalted be the God of my salvation.

New Testament Reading

Leader: God provides for our salvation by giving us his Son who lived as a human and, though sinless, died so that we who sin may have forgiveness and eternal life in heaven. Christ suffered on earth as part of his humanity. This means that we, too, will feel pain, sorrow, and suffering, a part of our humanity. Yet, we are assured of salvation by Christ's death, and fear, no longer has power over us. We read in Hebrews 2:6-18:

What are human beings that you are mindful of them, or mortals, that you care for them? You have made them for a little while lower than the angels; you have crowned them with glory and honor, subjecting all things under their feet. Now in subjecting all things to them, God left nothing outside their control. As it is, we do not yet see everything in subjection to them, but we do see Jesus, who for a little while was made lower than the angels, now crowned with glory and honor because of the suffering of death, so that by the grace of God he might taste death for everyone. It was fitting that God, for whom and through whom all things exist, in bringing many children to glory, should

make the pioneer of their salvation perfect through suf-
ferings. For the one who sanctifies and those who are
sanctified all have one Father.

We learn from this reading how God has cared for
us and guided us beyond our human comprehension.
Not only has God given us Jesus Christ, our redeemer,
but, as the reading continues, we see how Jesus has
made us one with him, as brothers and sisters — all of
us the children of God. We continue:

For this reason Jesus is not ashamed to call them
brothers and sisters, saying, "I will proclaim your name
to my brothers and sisters, in the midst of the congre-
gation I will praise you." And again, "I will put my
trust in him." And again, "Here am I and the children
whom God has given me." Since, therefore, the chil-
dren share flesh and blood, he himself likewise shared
the same things, so that through death he might de-
stroy the one who has the power of death, that is, the
devil, and free those who all their lives were held in
slavery by the fear of death. For it is clear that he did
not come to help angels, but the descendants of
Abraham. Therefore he had to become like his broth-
ers and sisters in every respect, so that he might be a
merciful and faithful high priest in the service of God,
to make a sacrifice of atonement for the sins of the
people. Because he himself was tested by what he suf-
fered, he is able to help those who are being tested.

Meditation and Prayer

Leader: When we lose a loved one, we do, indeed, feel tested.
We suffer and feel loneliness and sorrow. As we reflect upon the words read a few moments ago, we more
fully understand our suffering and the sacrifice made
for us by our Lord, Jesus Christ. Let us meditate on
these words. (*Silence*) Let us pray. Heavenly Father,
we know that as Christ suffered, we too suffer, but we
joy in the assurance that because you love your Son,

68

you love us. We have seen your steadfast love daily in our lives. We thank you for the sacrifice and love offered to us freely. We pray in Jesus' name. Amen.

Reading from the Gospel of John

Reader: Before Jesus ascended to heaven, he prepared the disciples. Jesus taught them all they needed to know to continue their work on earth. We, also, learn to understand God's promises to us, as we study the Word. We read what Jesus said in John 14:11-21:

Believe me that I am in the Father and the Father is in me; but if you do not, then believe me because of the works themselves. Very truly, I tell you, the one who believes in me will also do the works that I do and, in fact, will do greater works than these, because I am going to the Father. I will do whatever you ask in my name, so that the Father may be glorified in the Son. If in my name you ask me for anything, I will do it. If you love me, you will keep my commandments. And I will ask the Father, and he will give you another Advocate, to be with you forever. This is the Spirit of truth, whom the world cannot receive, because it neither sees him nor knows him. You know him, because he abides with you, and he will be in you. I will not leave you orphaned; I am coming to you. In a little while the world will no longer see me, but you will see me; because I live, you also will live. On that day you will know that I am in my Father, and you in me, and I in you. They who have my commandments and keep them are those who love me; and those who love me will be loved by my Father, and I will love them and reveal myself to them.

Leader: Jesus in his final days prepared the disciples for the work they were to do after he was gone. Our own lives reflect the discipleship which Jesus taught us — to be kind, compassionate, faithful, and loving. Let us meditate for a few moments on the discipleship of

69

_____ in your lives. (*Silence*) Remembering how _____ touched your life, we offer this time for you to share special memories or recollections with us.

A Time for Sharing
(*The leader will allow time for recollections.*)

Comfort for the Living
Reader: Before Jesus ascended, his prayer to God reminds us of the promise that God will continue to protect us and care for us. Although sadness fills you today, these words of Christ will offer you comfort and hope.

After Jesus had spoken these words, he looked up to heaven and said, "Father, the hour has come; glorify your Son so that the Son may glorify you, since you have given him authority over all people, to give eternal life to all whom you have given him. And this is eternal life, that they may know you, the only true God, and Jesus Christ whom you have sent. I glorified you on earth by finishing the work that you gave me to do. So now, Father, glorify me in your own presence with the glory that I had in your presence before the world existed. I have made your name known to those whom you gave me from the world. They were yours, and you gave them to me, and they have kept your word. Now they know that everything you have given me is from you; for the words that you gave to me I have given to them, and they have received them and know in truth that I came from you; and they have believed that you sent me. I am asking on their behalf; I am not asking on behalf of the world, but on behalf of those whom you gave me, because they are yours. All mine are yours, and yours are mine; and I have been glorified in them. And now I am no longer in the world, but they are in the world, and I am coming to you. Holy

70

Father, protect them in your name that you have given me, so that they may be one, as we are one (John 17:1-11).

Reading from Ephesians 2:17-22

Leader: As Jesus ascended he proclaimed peace to the world. Those of us who are gathered here today can be assured that God's peace is present in our lives. The Comforter, the Holy Spirit, will fill you with peace and love when you call upon him. Be assured that there is hope for all. Some day each of us will join the saints in heaven and will sit at the feet of Jesus where incomprehensible peace will be ours. Listen to God's Word.

So he came and proclaimed peace to you who were far off and peace to those who were near; for through him both of us have access in one Spirit to the Father. So then you are no longer strangers and aliens, but you are citizens with the saints and also members of the household of God, built upon the foundation of the apostles and prophets, with Christ Jesus himself as the cornerstone. In him the whole structure is joined together and grows into a holy temple in the Lord; in whom you also are built together spiritually into a dwelling place for God.

Responsive Reading from Isaiah 61:1-2

Reader: The spirit of the Lord God is upon me, because the Lord has anointed me;

Response: **He has sent me to bring good news to the oppressed,**

Reader: To bind up the brokenhearted,

Response: **To proclaim liberty to the captives, and release to the prisoners;**

Reader: To proclaim the year of the Lord's favor,

Response: **To comfort all who mourn.**

Leader: Let us pray the prayer that Jesus taught us:

All: **Our Father which art in heaven, hallowed be thy name. Thy kingdom come. Thy will be done in earth,**

71

as it is in heaven. **Give us this day our daily bread. And forgive us our debts, as we forgive our debtors. And lead us not into temptation, but deliver us from evil: For thine is the kingdom, and the power, and the glory, forever. Amen.**

Closing Prayer

Leader: Jesus' words of peace are familiar to us all. Let us conclude with these words from John 14:

Peace I leave with you; my peace I give to you. I do not give to you as the world gives. Do not let your hearts be troubled, and do not let them be afraid. You heard me say to you, I am going away, and I am coming to you. If you loved me, you would rejoice that I am going to the Father, because the Father is greater than I (John 14:27-28).

And if I go and prepare a place for you, I will come again and will take you to myself, so that where I am, there you may be also (John 14:3).

With that promise of hope and comfort, we thank and praise you, Lord God. We ask you to be with all of those who mourn providing them with strength and your steadfast love. In Jesus' name we pray. Amen.

(The service is concluded.)

In My Father's House

(The participants will read the portions of the service material marked **Response** *and* **All**.*)*

Opening Invocation

Responsive Reading from Psalm 145, selected verses

Reader: I will extol you, my God and King, and bless your name forever and ever.

Response: Every day I will bless you, and praise your name forever and ever.

Reader: Great is the Lord, and greatly to be praised; his greatness is unsearchable.

Response: One generation shall laud your works to another, and shall declare your mighty acts.

Reader: They shall celebrate the fame of your abundant goodness, and shall sing aloud of your righteousness.

Response: The Lord is gracious and merciful, slow to anger and abounding in steadfast love.

Reader: The Lord is good to all, and his compassion is over all that he has made.

Response: They shall speak of the glory of your kingdom, and tell of your power,

Reader: Your kingdom is an everlasting kingdom, and your dominion endures throughout all generations.

Response: The Lord is faithful in all his words, and gracious in all his deeds.

Reader: The Lord upholds all who are falling, and raises up all who are bowed down.

Response: The eyes of all look to you, and you give them their food in due season.

Reader: The Lord is near to all who call on him, to all who call on him in truth.

Response: The Lord watches over all who love him, but all the wicked he will destroy.

All: **My mouth will speak the praise of the Lord, and all flesh will bless his holy name forever and ever.**

Prayer

Old Testament Responsive Reading from Psalm 18:30-32, 35, 46

Reader: This God — his way is perfect; the promise of the Lord proves true; he is a shield for all who take refuge in him.

Response: **For who is God except the Lord?**

Reader: And who is a rock besides our God? — the God who girded me with strength, and made my way safe.

Response: **You have given me the shield of your salvation, and your right hand has supported me; your help has made me great.**

All: **The Lord lives! Blessed be my rock, and exalted be the God of my salvation.**

New Testament Reading

Meditation and Prayer

Reading from the Gospel of John 17:11-21

A Time for Sharing

Comfort for the Living

Reading from Ephesians 2:17-22

Responsive Reading from Isaiah 61:1-2

Reader: The spirit of the Lord God is upon me, because the Lord has anointed me;

Response: He has sent me to bring good news to the oppressed,
Reader: To bind up the brokenhearted,
Response: To proclaim liberty to the captives, and release to the prisoners;
Reader: To proclaim the year of the Lord's favor,
Response: To comfort all who mourn.

The Lord's Prayer
All: Our Father which art in heaven, hallowed be thy name. Thy kingdom come. Thy will be done in earth, as it is in heaven. Give us this day our daily bread. And forgive us our debts, as we forgive our debtors. And lead us not into temptation, but deliver us from evil: For thine is the kingdom, and the power, and the glory, forever. Amen.

Closing Prayer

Service 7

I Am The Bread Of Life

(Family and friends are called to silence for the opening of the prayer service.)

Opening Invocation

Leader: In the name of the Father and of the Son and of the Holy Spirit. Amen.

Jesus said, "I am the bread of life. Whoever comes to me will never be hungry, and whoever believes in me will never be thirsty. This is the will of him who sent me, that I should lose nothing of all that he has given me, but raise it upon the last day" (John 6:35, 39).

Today we celebrate the life and death of _____ who has been raised up to live with God in heaven. In the wondrous gift of the Bread of Life, we receive the gift of eternal life.

Responsive Reading from Philippians 4:4-7

Reader: Rejoice in the Lord always; again I will say, Rejoice.

Response: Let your gentleness be known to everyone. The Lord is near.

Reader: Do not worry about anything, but in everything by prayer and supplication with thanksgiving let your requests be made known to God.

Response: And the peace of God, which surpasses all understanding, will guard your hearts and your minds in Christ Jesus.

Prayer

Leader: Let us pray. Heavenly Father, you have given us the Bread of life. You feed our bodies with manna from heaven and you feed our souls with the Bread of Life from heaven. We thank you for these gifts. Open our ears to your Word that we may find hope and comfort for those who mourn. Help us to remember that your steadfast love and mercy is free to all who call upon you. In your name we pray. Amen.

Old Testament Responsive Reading from Isaiah 55:10-13, 56:1

Reader: For as the rain and the snow come down from heaven, and do not return there until they have watered the earth,

Response: Making it bring forth and sprout, giving seed to the sower and bread to the eater,

Reader: So shall my word be that goes out from my mouth; it shall not return to me empty,

Response: But it shall accomplish that which I purpose, and succeed in the thing for which I sent it.

Reader: For you shall go out in joy, and be led back in peace;

Response: The mountains and the hills before you shall burst into song, and all the trees of the field shall clap their hands.

Reader: Instead of the thorn shall come up the cypress; instead of the brier shall come up the myrtle;

Response: And it shall be to the Lord for a memorial, for an everlasting sign that shall not be cut off.

Reader: Thus says the Lord: Maintain justice, and do what is right,

Response: For soon my salvation will come, and my deliverance be revealed.

New Testament Readings

Leader: *Our ancestors ate the manna in the wilderness; as it is written, "He gave them bread from heaven to eat." Then Jesus said to them, "Very truly, I tell you, it was not Moses who gave you the bread from heaven, but it is my Father who gives you the true bread from heaven. For the bread of God is that which comes down from heaven and gives life to the world." They said to him, "Sir, give us this bread always." Jesus said to them, "I* *am the bread of life. Whoever comes to me will never be hungry, and whoever believes in me will never be thirsty. But I say to you that you have seen me and yet do not believe. Everything that the Father gives me will come to me, and anyone who comes to me I will never drive away; for I have come down from heaven, not to do my own will, but the will of him who sent me. And this is the will of him who sent me, that I should lose nothing of all that he has given me, but raise it up on the last day. This is indeed the will of my Father, that all who see the Son and believe in him may have eternal life; and I will raise them up on the last day"* (John 6:31-39).

Communion is a celebration of Jesus, our Bread of Life. As we commune, we remember that Jesus suffered death and rose again to heaven to prepare a place for us. As we drink the wine and eat the earthly bread, we do this in remembrance of Jesus, our Bread of Life. We read in Matthew 26:26-29:

While they were eating, Jesus took a loaf of bread, and after blessing it he broke it, gave it to the disciples, and said, "Take, eat; this is my body." Then he took a cup, and after giving thanks he gave it to them, saying, "Drink from it, all of you; for this is my blood of the covenant, which is poured out for many for the forgiveness of sins. I tell you, I will never again drink of this fruit of the vine until that day when I drink it new with you in my Father's kingdom."

Responsive Reading

Leader: God, our Father, in his mercy gave us his only Son, our Savior, Jesus Christ, so that we may have eternal life for all who believe. We read responsively in John 3:31-36:

Reader: The one who comes from above is above all; the one who is of the earth belongs to the earth and speaks about earthly things.

Response: The one who comes from heaven is above all.

Reader: He testifies to what he has seen and heard,

Response: Yet no one accepts his testimony.

Reader: Whoever has accepted his testimony has certified this, that God is true.

Response: He whom God has sent speaks the words of God, for he gives the Spirit without measure.

Reader: The Father loves the Son and has placed all things in his hands.

Response: Whoever believes in the Son has eternal life.

Meditation and Prayer

Leader: In God's mercy, salvation was planned for us. Let us reflect upon the words read a few moments ago. (*Silence*) We pray, Heavenly Father, you provide us with all needs of the body and soul. You give eternal life to all who believe in Jesus Christ, the Bread of Life and Savior of the world. We give you thanks and praise. May your peace fill our hearts and minds. In Jesus' name. Amen.

Reading from Philippians 3:13-18, 20-21

Reader: What have we done to deserve this gift from God? What does God expect of us? How should we live our lives? We read Paul's answer in Philippians 3:

Beloved, I do not consider that I have made it my own; but this one thing I do: forgetting what lies behind and straining forward to what lies ahead, I press on toward the goal for the prize of the heavenly call of God in Christ Jesus. Let those of us then who are mature be of the same mind; and if you think differently about anything, this too God will reveal to you. Only let us hold fast to what we have attained. Brothers and sisters, join in imitating me, and observe those who live according to the example you have in us. For many live as enemies of the cross of Christ; I have often told you of them, and now I tell you even with tears. But our citizenship is in heaven, and it is from there that we are expecting a Savior, the Lord Jesus Christ. He will transform the body of our humiliation that it may be conformed to the body of his glory, by the power that also enables him to make all things subject to himself.

Leader: As Paul tells us, we are to press on, to live our lives as God commands and as an example to the world. Let us take a few moments to recall the life of _____. As friends and family, you remember the joys, sorrows, and daily experiences you shared with him/her. (*Silence*) As you recall these memories, you are asked if there are any that you would like to share with family and friends at this time, remembering the way in which _____ touched your life.

A Time for Sharing
(*The leader will allow time for recollections.*)

Comfort for the Living

Reader: *Jesus said: "This is indeed the will of my Father, that all who see the Son and believe in him may have eternal life; and I will raise them up on the last day. Very truly, I tell you, whoever believes has eternal life. I am the bread of life. Your ancestors ate the manna in the wilderness, and they died. This is the bread that comes down from heaven, so that one may eat of it and not die. I am the living bread that came down from heaven. Whoever eats of this bread will live forever; and the bread that I will give for the life of the world is my flesh, and I will raise them up on the last day; for my flesh is true food and my blood is true drink. Those who eat my flesh and drink my blood abide in me, and I in them. Just as the living Father sent me, and I live because of the Father, so whoever eats me will live because of me. This is the bread that came down from heaven, not like that which your ancestors ate, and* *they died. But the one who eats this bread will live forever"* (John 6:40, 47-51, 54-58).

Leader: Jesus has assured us that through him we have eternal life, in the beautiful words of John 3:16-17: "For God so loved that world that he gave his only Son, so that everyone who believes in him may not perish but may have eternal life. Indeed, God did not send the Son into the world to condemn the world, but in order that the world might be saved through him." We are assured that today _____ lives in God's heavenly kingdom.

Responsive Reading from Luke 11:9-13

Leader: The book of Deuteronomy is the final book of the law and is associated with Moses. In Deuteronomy 8:3, Moses speaks to the people, "[God] humbled you by letting you hunger, then by feeding you with manna, with which neither you nor your ancestors were acquainted, in order to make you understand that one does not live by bread alone, but by every word that comes from the mouth of the Lord." This verse emphasizes through God's Word we receive hope, comfort, and the assurance of everlasting life. Let us read responsively:

Reader: So I say to you, Ask, and it will be given you; search, and you will find;

Response: Knock, and the door will be opened for you.

Reader: For everyone who asks receives, and everyone who searches finds,

Response: And for everyone who knocks, the door will be opened.

Reader: Is there anyone among you who, if your child asks for a fish, will give a snake instead of a fish?

Response: Or if the child asks for an egg, will give a scorpion?

Reader: If you then, who are evil, know how to give good gifts to your children,

Response: How much more will the heavenly Father give the Holy Spirit to those who ask him!

Leader: Let us pray the pray our Lord taught us:

All: **Our Father which art in heaven, hallowed be thy name. Thy kingdom come. Thy will be done in earth, as it is in heaven. Give us this day our daily bread. And forgive us our debts, as we forgive our debtors. And lead us not into temptation, but deliver us from evil: For thine is the kingdom, and the power, and the glory, for ever. Amen.**

Closing Prayer

Leader: Jesus said, "I am the living bread that came down from heaven. Whoever eats of this bread will live forever; and the bread that I will give for the life of the world is my flesh. Those who eat my flesh and drink my blood have eternal life, and I will raise them up on the last day." Heavenly Father, we are grateful for your gifts to us. Our simple prayers of thankfulness cannot express the joy and comfort we receive with your assurance that we and all believers will someday join _____ and all our loved ones in heaven. Grant us your steadfast love, and may the Holy Spirit comfort us in the days ahead. In the name of Jesus, our Bread of Life, Amen.

(The service is concluded.)

I Am The Bread Of Life

(The participants will read the portions of the service marked with **Response** *and* **All.***)*

Opening Invocation

Responsive Reading Philippians 4:4-7
Reader: Rejoice in the Lord always; again I will say, Rejoice.
Response: Let your gentleness be known to everyone. The Lord is near.
Reader: Do not worry about anything, but in everything by prayer and supplication with thanksgiving let your requests be made known to God.
Response: And the peace of God, which surpasses all understanding, will guard your hearts and your minds in Christ Jesus.

Prayer

Old Testament Responsive Reading from Isaiah 55:10-13; 56:1
Reader: For as the rain and the snow come down from heaven, and do not return there until they have watered the earth,
Response: Making it bring forth and sprout, giving seed to the sower and bread to the eater,
Reader: So shall my word be that goes out from my mouth; it shall not return to me empty,
Response: But it shall accomplish that which I purpose, and succeed in the thing for which I sent it.
Reader: For you shall go out in joy, and be led back in peace;
Response: The mountains and the hills before you shall burst into song, and all the trees of the field shall clap their hands.

Reader:	Instead of the thorn shall come up the cypress; instead of the brier shall come up the myrtle;
Response:	**And it shall be to the Lord for a memorial, for an everlasting sign that shall not be cut off.**
Reader:	Thus says the Lord: Maintain justice, and do what is right,
Response:	**For soon my salvation will come, and my deliverance be revealed.**

New Testament Readings from John 6:31-39; Matthew 26:26-29

Responsive Reading from John 3:31-36

Reader:	The one who comes from above is above all; the one who is of the earth belongs to the earth and speaks about earthly things.
Response:	**The one who comes from heaven is above all.**
Reader:	He testifies to what he has seen and heard,
Response:	**Yet no one accepts his testimony.**
Reader:	Whoever has accepted his testimony has certified this, that God is true.
Response:	**He whom God has sent speaks the words of God, for he gives the Spirit without measure.**
Reader:	The Father loves the Son and has placed all things in his hands.
Response:	**Whoever believes in the Son has eternal life.**

Meditation and Prayer

Reading from Philippians 3:13-18, 20-21

A Time for Sharing

Comfort for the Living

Responsive Reading from Luke 11:9-13

Reader: So I say to you, Ask, and it will be given you; search, and you will find;

Response: Knock, and the door will be opened for you.

Reader: For everyone who asks receives, and everyone who searches finds,

Response: And for everyone who knocks, the door will be opened.

Reader: Is there anyone among you who, if your child asks for a fish, will give a snake instead of a fish?

Response: Or if the child asks for an egg, will give a scorpion?

Reader: If you then, who are evil, know how to give good gifts to your children,

Response: How much more will the heavenly Father give the Holy Spirit to those who ask him!

The Lord's Prayer

All: **Our Father which art in heaven, hallowed be thy name. Thy kingdom come. Thy will be done in earth, as it is in heaven. Give us this day our daily bread. And forgive us our debts, as we forgive our debtors. And lead us not into temptation, but deliver us from evil: For thine is the kingdom, and the power, and the glory, for ever. Amen.**

Closing Prayer

Service 8

I Am The True Vine

(Family and friends are called to silence for the opening of the prayer service.)

Opening Invocation

Leader: We begin in the name of the Father and of the Son and of the Holy Spirit. Amen.

I am he who comforts you; why then are you afraid of a mere mortal who must die, a human being who fades like grass? You have forgotten the Lord, your Maker, who stretched out the heavens and laid the foundations of the earth (Isaiah 51:12-13).

Though we are like grass that fades and withers, Jesus assures us, as an extension of him, we will endure. Jesus says, "I am the true vine, you are the branches." Today we celebrate the victory of _____ who has overcome death and as a branch of the true vine continues to live eternally, abiding in God's love in heaven.

Responsive Reading from Psalm 102:11-13, 18-20

Reader: My days are like an evening shadow;

Response: I wither away like grass.

Reader: But you, O Lord, are enthroned forever;

Response: Your name endures to all generations.

Reader: You will rise up and have compassion on Zion, for it is time to favor it;

Response: The appointed time has come.

Reader: Let this be recorded for a generation to come,

Response: So that a people yet unborn may praise the Lord:

Reader: That he looked down from his holy height,

Response: From heaven the Lord looked at the earth,

Reader: To hear the groans of the prisoners,

Response: To set free those who were doomed to die.

87

Prayer

Leader: Lord, our God, though we are like grass that withers and fades, you nourish us and water us with your Word. May we learn to drink from the cup of forgiveness, so that we may become a living branch that will endure forever. In Jesus' name. Amen.

Old Testament Responsive Reading

Leader: Grass turns brown and withers from heat and lack of water, but it springs forth again when nourished. So we, too, are dead and lifeless without the renewing waters of the Word and the gardener, our Lord, who cares for our needs. We read in Psalm 90:1-9, 12-14:

Reader: Lord, you have been our dwelling place in all generations.

Response: Before the mountains were brought forth, or ever you had formed the earth and the world, from everlasting to everlasting you are God.

Reader: You turn us back to dust, and say, "Turn back, you mortals."

Response: For a thousand years in your sight are like yesterday when it is past, or like a watch in the night.

Reader: You sweep them away; they are like a dream, like grass that is renewed in the morning;

Response: In the morning it flourishes and is renewed; in the evening it fades and withers.

Reader: For we are consumed by your anger; by your wrath we are overwhelmed.

Response: You have set our iniquities before you, our secret sins in the light of your countenance.

Reader: For all our days pass away under your wrath; our years come to an end like a sigh.

Response: So teach us to count our days that we may gain a wise heart.

Reader: Turn, O Lord! How long? Have compassion on your servants!

Response: Satisfy us in the morning with your steadfast love, so that we may rejoice and be glad all our days.

New Testament Readings

Leader: We, like the green plants of earth, need the Light of God's countenance, the Water of the Word, and the Dew of God's love. Through these gifts, we are born anew each day — perishable, but imperishable — through the death and resurrection of the True Vine, our Lord, Jesus Christ. Listen to the message in 1 Peter 1:18-25:

You know that you were ransomed from the futile ways inherited from your ancestors, not with perishable things like silver or gold, but with the precious blood of Christ, like that of a lamb without defect or blemish. He was destined before the foundation of the world, but was revealed at the end of the ages for your sake. Through him you have come to trust in God, who raised him from the dead and gave him glory, so that your faith and hope are set on God. Now that you have purified your souls by your obedience to the truth so that you have genuine mutual love, love one another deeply from the heart. You have been born anew, not of perishable but of imperishable seed, through the living and enduring word of God. "All flesh is like grass and all its glory like the flower of grass. The grass withers, and the flower falls, but the word of the Lord endures forever."

Meditation and Prayer

Leader: In confidence, let us meditate in silence on these words, "You have been born anew, not of perishable, but imperishable seed, through the living and enduring word of God." (*Silence*) Let us pray. Lord, you give us hope and comfort in your Word. We thank you for the gifts which you provide daily. We pray in Jesus' name. Amen.

Continued Reading from 1 Peter 1:24—2:5

"All flesh is like grass and all its glory like the flower of grass. The grass withers, and the flower falls, but

the word of the Lord endures forever." That word is the
good news that was announced to you. Rid yourselves,
therefore, of all malice, and all guile, insincerity, envy,
and all slander. Like newborn infants, long for the pure,
spiritual milk, so that by it you may grow into salva-
tion — if indeed you have tasted that the Lord is good.
Come to him, a living stone, though rejected by mor-
tals yet chosen and precious in God's sight, and like
living stones, let yourselves be built into a spiritual
house, to be a holy priesthood, to offer spiritual sacri-
fices acceptable to God through Jesus Christ.

Leader: With the Good News in our hearts, we are commanded
to lead a life reflecting our gifts from God, as a testimony to our salvation. We who are chosen and precious in God's sight are asked to return to the world
gifts given to us. We are reminded of the way in which
_____ touched our lives, giving back to the world
gifts from God. You are asked to take a few moments
of silence to remember the life of _____. (*Si-*
lence) This time has been set aside for any of you who
desire to share with other members of the family and
friends, memories that illustrate a special way in which
_____ touched your life.

A Time for Sharing
(*The leader will allow time for recollections.*)

Comfort for the Living
Reader: From the beginning of time, God had our purpose in
mind. Rich or poor, old or young, beautiful or plain,
we are God's children, commanded to obey, yet offered forgiveness for our weakness and eternal life for
our faith.

If any of you is lacking in wisdom, ask God, who
gives to all generously and ungrudgingly, and it will
be given you. But ask in faith, never doubting, for the
one who doubts is like a wave of the sea, driven and

tossed by the wind; for the doubter, being double-minded and unstable in every way, must not expect to receive anything from the Lord. Let the believer who is lowly boast in being raised up, and the rich in being brought low, because the rich will disappear like a flower in the field. For the sun rises with its scorching heat and withers the field; its flower falls, and its beauty perishes. It is the same way with the rich; in the midst of a busy life, they will wither away. Blessed is anyone who endures temptation. Such a one has stood the test and will receive the crown of life that the Lord has promised to those who love him. No one, when tempted, should say, "I am being tempted by God"; for God cannot be tempted by evil and he himself tempts no one. But one is tempted by one's own desire, being lured and enticed by it; then, when that desire has conceived, it gives birth to sin, and that sin, when it is fully grown, gives birth to death. Do not be deceived, my beloved. Every generous act of giving, with every perfect gift, is from above, coming down from the Father of lights, with whom there is no variation or shadow due to change. In fulfillment of his own purpose he gave us birth by the word of truth, so that we would become a kind of first fruits of his creatures (James 1:5-18).

Reading from John 15:1-11

Leader: *I am the true vine, and my Father is the vinegrower. He removes every branch in me that bears no fruit. Every branch that bears fruit he prunes to make it bear more fruit. You have already been cleansed by the word that I have spoken to you. Abide in me as I abide in you. Just as the branch cannot bear fruit by itself unless it abides in the vine, neither can you unless you abide in me. I am the vine, you are the branches. Those who abide in me and I in them bear much fruit, because apart from me you can do nothing. Whoever does*

91

not abide in me is thrown away like a branch and with-
ers; such branches are gathered, thrown into the fire,
and burned. If you abide in me, and my words abide in
you, ask for whatever you wish, and it will be done for
you. My Father is glorified by this, that you bear much
fruit and become my disciples. As the Father has loved
me, so I have loved you; abide in my love. If you keep
my commandments, you will abide in my love, just as I
have kept my Father's commandments and abide in
his love. I have said these things to you so that my joy
may be in you, and that your joy may be complete.

Responsive Reading

Leader: Jesus has promised us whatever we ask in love and faithfulness, it will be done for us. Today we ask for comfort and compassion for those who mourn. We read responsively in Psalm 103:

Reader: As a father has compassion for his children,

Response: So the Lord has compassion for those who fear him.

Reader: For he knows how we were made;

Response: He remembers that we are dust.

Reader: As for mortals, their days are like grass;

Response: They flourish like a flower of the field;

Reader: For the wind passes over it, and it is gone,

Response: And its place knows it no more.

Reader: But the steadfast love of the Lord is from everlasting to everlasting on those who fear him, and his righteousness to children's children,

Response: To those who keep his covenant and remember to do his commandments.

Leader: Let us pray the prayer that our Lord taught us:

All: Our Father which art in heaven, hallowed be thy name. Thy kingdom come. Thy will be done in earth, as it is in heaven. Give us this day our daily bread. And forgive us our debts, as we forgive our debt-ors. And lead us not into temptation, but deliver us from evil: For thine is the kingdom, and the power, and the glory, for ever. Amen.

Closing Prayer

Leader: *A mortal born of woman, few of days and full of trouble, comes up like a flower and withers, flees like a shadow and does not last. Do you fix your eyes on such a one? There is hope in a tree, if it is cut down, that it will sprout again, and that its shoots will not cease. Though its root grows old in the earth, and its stump dies in the ground, yet a scent of water it will bud and put forth branches like a young plant* (Job 14:1-3, 7-9).

We find hope and comfort in the assurance that _____ lives, like a new shoot in heaven, a branch from the Stump of Jesse. We pray that we, too, will not fade and wither, but when our day comes, we will also blossom in newness of life with all the saints in heaven. We thank and praise you, Lord, and ask you to continue to water us with your Word and comfort us with the presence of the Holy Spirit. We pray in the name of Jesus. Amen.

(The service is concluded.)

I Am The True Vine

(The participants will read the portions of the service marked **Response** *and* **All**.*)*

Opening Invocation

Responsive Reading from Psalm 102:11-13, 18-20
Reader: My days are like an evening shadow;
Response: **I wither away like grass.**
Reader: But you, O Lord, are enthroned forever;
Response: **Your name endures to all generations.**
Reader: You will rise up and have compassion on Zion, for it is time to favor it;
Response: **The appointed time has come.**
Reader: Let this be recorded for a generation to come,
Response: **So that a people yet unborn may praise the Lord:**
Reader: That he looked down from his holy height,
Response: **From heaven the Lord looked at the earth,**
Reader: To hear the groans of the prisoners,
Response: **To set free those who were doomed to die.**

Prayer

Old Testament Responsive Reading from Psalm 90:1-9, 12-14
Reader: Lord, you have been our dwelling place in all generations.
Response: **Before the mountains were brought forth, or ever you had formed the earth and the world, from everlasting to everlasting you are God.**
Reader: You turn us back to dust, and say, "Turn back, you mortals."
Response: **For a thousand years in your sight are like yesterday when it is past, or like a watch in the night.**

94

Reader: You sweep them away; they are like a dream, like grass that is renewed in the morning;

Response: In the morning it flourishes and is renewed; in the evening it fades and withers.

Reader: For we are consumed by your anger; by your wrath we are overwhelmed.

Response: You have set our iniquities before you, our secret sins in the light of your countenance.

Reader: For all our days pass away under your wrath; our years come to an end like a sigh.

Response: So teach us to count our days that we may gain a wise heart.

Reader: Turn, O Lord! How long? Have compassion on your servants!

Response: Satisfy us in the morning with your steadfast love, so that we may rejoice and be glad all our days.

New Testament Reading from 1 Peter 1:18-25

Prayer and Meditation

Reading from 1 Peter 1:24—2:5

A Time for Sharing

Comfort for the Living

Reading from John 15:1-11

Responsive Reading from Psalm 103:13-18
Reader: As a father has compassion for his children,
Response: So the Lord has compassion for those who fear him.
Reader: For he knows how we were made;
Response: He remembers that we are dust.
Reader: As for mortals, their days are like grass;
Response: They flourish like a flower of the field;

Reader: For the wind passes over it, and it is gone,

Response: And its place knows it no more.

Reader: But the steadfast love of the Lord is from everlasting to everlasting on those who fear him, and his righteousness to children's children,

Response: To those who keep his covenant and remember to do his commandments.

The Lord's Prayer

All: Our Father which art in heaven, hallowed be thy name. Thy kingdom come. Thy will be done in earth, as it is in heaven. Give us this day our daily bread. And forgive us our debts, as we forgive our debtors. And lead us not into temptation, but deliver us from evil: For thine is the kingdom, and the power, and the glory, for ever. Amen.

Closing Prayer

Service 9

Child Of God, Heir To The Kingdom

(Family and friends are called to silence for the opening of the prayer service.)

Opening Invocation
Leader: In the name of the Father and the Son and the Holy Spirit. Amen.

Because you are children, God has sent the Spirit of his Son into our hearts, crying, "Abba Father!" So you are no longer a slave but a child, and if a child then also an heir, through God (Galatians 4:6-7).

Today we celebrate the victory of _____, a child of God and heir to kingdom. We are assured that _____ lives with God in a heavenly mansion prepared for each of us. We thank you, Father, for making us your own and giving us eternal life with you in heaven.

Responsive Reading from 1 John 5:1-6
Reader: Everyone who believes that Jesus is the Christ has been born of God,
Response: **And everyone who loves the parent loves the child.**
Reader: By this we know that we love the children of God,
Response: **When we love God and obey his commandments.**
Reader: For the love of God is this, that we obey his commandments.
Response: **And his commandments are not burdensome,**
Reader: For whatever is born of God conquers the world.
Response: **And this is the victory that conquers the world, our faith.**
Reader: Who is it that conquers the world but the one who believes that Jesus is the Son of God?

Response: **This is the one who came by water and blood, Jesus Christ, not with the water only but with the water and the blood. And the Spirit is the one that testifies, for the Spirit is the truth.**

Prayer
Leader: Heavenly Father, you give us life and made us heirs to your kingdom through the death and resurrection of your Son and our Brother, Jesus Christ. We give you thanks and praise for your mercy. Help to comfort those who grieve and help us understand that death is the gift of life, a journey home to live with the Father and brothers and sisters in the faith who have gone on before us. In his name we pray. Amen.

Old Testament Responsive Reading from Psalm 103:8-18

Reader: The Lord is merciful and gracious, slow to anger and abounding in steadfast love.

Response: **He will not always accuse, nor will he keep his anger forever.**

Reader: He does not deal with us according to our sins, nor repay us according to our iniquities.

Response: **For as the heavens are high above the earth, so great is his steadfast love toward those who fear him;**

Reader: As far as the east is from the west, so far he removes our transgressions from us.

Response: **As a father has compassion for his children, so the Lord has compassion for those who fear him.**

Reader: For he knows how we were made; he remembers that we are dust.

Response: **As for mortals, their days are like grass; they flourish like a flower of the field; for the wind passes over it, and it is gone, and its place knows it no more.**

Reader: But the steadfast love of the Lord is from everlasting to everlasting on those who fear him, and his righteousness to children's children,

Response: **To those who keep his covenant and remember to do his commandments.**

New Testament Readings

Leader: God, our Father and Creator, like an earthly father, cares for us and guides us, but the greatest gift is we are his children and heirs to his kingdom. We read this in Galatians 3:26—4:7:

In Christ Jesus you are all children of God through faith. As many of you as were baptized into Christ have clothed yourselves with Christ (1 Corinthians 5:20-26) *... All of you are one in Christ Jesus. And if you belong to Christ, then you are Abraham's offspring, heirs according to the promise. My point is this: heirs, as long as they are minors, are no better than slaves, though they are the owners of all the property; but they remain under guardians and trustees until the date set by the father. So with us; while we were minors, we were enslaved to the elemental spirits of the world. But when the fullness of time had come, God sent his Son, born of a woman, born under the law, in order to redeem those who were under the law, so that we might receive adoption as children. And because you are children, God has sent the Spirit of his Son into our hearts, crying, "Abba! Father!" So you are no longer a slave but a child, and if a child then also an heir, through God.*

Reader: As children of God, we are heirs in heaven, but we also must suffer as Christ has suffered. Our sorrow, loneliness, and pain are all part of our oneness with Christ who suffered on earth to gain for us a place in heaven. Listen to Roman 8:14-28:

For all who are led by the Spirit of God are children of God. For you did not receive a spirit of slavery to fall back into fear, but you have received a spirit of adoption. When we cry, "Abba! Father!" it is that very Spirit bearing witness with our spirit that we are children of God, and if children, then heirs, heirs of God and joint heirs with Christ — if, in fact, we suffer with him so that we may also be glorified with him. I consider that the sufferings of this present time are not worth comparing with the glory about to be revealed to us. For the creation waits with eager longing for the revealing of the children of God; for the creation was subjected to futility, not of its own will but by the will of the one who subjected it, in hope, that the creation itself will be set free from its bondage to decay and will obtain the freedom of the glory of the children of God. We know that the whole creation has been groaning in labor pains until now; and not only the creation, but we ourselves, who have the first fruits of the Spirit, groan inwardly while we wait for adoption, the redemption of our bodies. For in hope we were saved. Now hope that is seen is not hope. For who hopes for what is seen? But if we hope for what we do not see, we wait for it with patience. Likewise the Spirit helps us in our weakness; for we do not know how to pray as we ought, but that very Spirit intercedes with sighs too deep for words. And God, who searches the heart, knows what is the mind of the Spirit, because the Spirit intercedes for the saints according to the will of God. We know that all things work together for good for those who love God, who are called according to his purpose.

Responsive Reading from John 14:1-4

Leader: There is comfort in knowing the Holy Spirit intercedes for us and God knows what is in our hearts. We also are comforted by the words of Jesus, read responsively:

Reader: Do not let your hearts be troubled.

Response: Believe in God, believe also in me.

Reader: In my Father's house there are many dwelling places.

Response: If it were not so, would I have told you that I go to prepare a place for you?

Reader: And if I go and prepare a place for you, I will come again and will take you to myself,

Response: So that where I am, there you may be also.

Meditation and Prayer

Leader: *[God] destined us for adoption as his children through Jesus Christ, according to the good pleasure of his will, to the praise of his glorious grace that he freely bestowed on us ... In him, we have redemption through his blood, the forgiveness of our trespasses, according to the riches of his grace that he lavished on us. With all wisdom and insight he has made known to us ... a plan for the fullness of time, to gather up all things in him, things in heaven and things on earth* (Ephesians 1:5-10).

With the joy of this reality in mind, let us silently reflect upon these words. (*Silence*) Let us pray. Heavenly Father, through your Son, we have inherited the kingdom of heaven. You have given us the Holy Spirit, the comforter, and we thank you for these gifts. Help us to understand and to accept the sorrow and suffering which we must bear on earth. May we eagerly await the promised mansions awaiting us in heaven. In Jesus' name we pray. Amen.

Reading from John 13:33-35

Leader: Before Jesus ascended to heaven, he said:

Little children, I am with you only a little longer. You will look for me; and as I said to the Jews so now I say to you, "Where I am going, you cannot come." I give you a new commandment, that you love one another. Just as I have loved you, you also should love one another. By this everyone will know that you are my disciples, if you have love for one another."

We were commanded by Jesus to show the world that we are children of God, by extending love, compassion, kindness, and patience to one another. Each of you will recall times when _____ offered you love, guidance, generosity, or in some way made an impact on your life. Let us take a few moments of silence to think about those expressions of

101

love. (*Silence*) This would be a fitting time to share any of those memories with the family and friends gathered here today.

A Time for Sharing
(*The leader will allow time for recollections.*)

Comfort for the Living
Reader: *See what love the Father has given us, that we should be called children of God; and that is what we are. The reason the world does not know us is that it did not know him. Beloved, we are God's children now; what we will be has not yet been revealed. What we do know is this: when he is revealed, we will be like him, for we will see him as he is. And all who have this hope in him purify themselves, just as he is pure. We know that we have passed from death to life because we love one another. Whoever does not love abides in death. We know love by this, that he laid down his life for us — and we ought to lay down our lives for one another. Beloved, let us love one another, because love is from God; everyone who loves is born of God and knows God. Whoever does not love does not know God, for God is love. God's love was revealed among us in this way: God sent his only Son into the world so that we might live through him. In this is love, not that we loved God but that he loved us and sent his Son to be the atoning sacrifice for our sins* (1 John 3:1-3, 14, 16; 4:7-10).

Responsive Reading from Matthew 18:3-5, 10; Mark 10:14-16
Leader: Jesus loved the little children. Jesus loves us. He willingly gave his life for us. Jesus reminds us that we must have faith like a child, not only a child of God, but a small child who does not doubt or question, but who accepts God's Word and salvation.

102

Reader: Truly I tell you, unless you change and become like children, you will never enter the kingdom of heaven.

Response: Whoever becomes humble like this child is the greatest in the kingdom of heaven.

Reader: Whoever welcomes one such child in my name welcomes me. Take care that you do not despise one of these little ones;

Response: For, I tell you, in heaven their angels continually see the face of my Father in heaven.

Reader: Let the little children come to me; do not stop them;

Response: For it is to such as these that the kingdom of God belongs.

Reader: Truly I tell you, whoever does not receive the kingdom of God as a little child will never enter it.

Response: And he took them up in his arms, laid his hands on them, and blessed them.

Leader: Let us pray the prayer that our Lord taught us:

All: Our Father which art in heaven, hallowed be thy name. Thy kingdom come. Thy will be done in earth, as it is in heaven. Give us this day our daily bread. And forgive us our debts, as we forgive our debtors. And lead us not into temptation, but deliver us from evil: For thine is the kingdom, and the power, and the glory, for ever. Amen.

Closing Prayer

Leader: We thank you, God, for your Son, our Brother, who gave his life for us, so that we are heirs to the heavenly kingdom. Father, hold us in your protective arms, wipe our tears, and help us to understand the joy that is ours in heaven. We pray this in the name of him who gave his life for us. Amen.

(The service is concluded.)

Child Of God, Heir To The Kingdom

(The participants will read the portions of the service marked **Response** *and* **All.***)*

Opening Invocation

Responsive Reading from 1 John 5:1-6
Reader: Everyone who believes that Jesus is the Christ has been born of God,
Response: And everyone who loves the parent loves the child.
Reader: By this we know that we love the children of God,
Response: When we love God and obey his commandments.
Reader: For the love of God is this, that we obey his commandments.
Response: And his commandments are not burdensome,
Reader: For whatever is born of God conquers the world.
Response: And this is the victory that conquers the world, our faith.
Reader: Who is it that conquers the world but the one who believes that Jesus is the Son of God?
Response: This is the one who came by water and blood, Jesus Christ, not with the water only but with the water and the blood. And the Spirit is the one that testifies, for the Spirit is the truth.

Prayer

Old Testament Responsive Reading from Psalm 103:8-18
Reader: The Lord is merciful and gracious, slow to anger and abounding in steadfast love.
Response: He will not always accuse, nor will he keep his anger forever.

104

Reader:	He does not deal with us according to our sins, nor repay us according to our iniquities.
Response:	**For as the heavens are high above the earth, so great is his steadfast love toward those who fear him;**
Reader:	As far as the east is from the west, so far he removes our transgressions from us.
Response:	**As a father has compassion for his children, so the Lord has compassion for those who fear him.**
Reader:	For he knows how we were made; he remembers that we are dust.
Response:	**As for mortals, their days are like grass; they flourish like a flower of the field; for the wind passes over it, and it is gone, and its place knows it no more.**
Reader:	But the steadfast love of the Lord is from everlasting to everlasting on those who fear him, and his righteousness to children's children,
Response:	**To those who keep his covenant and remember to do his commandments.**

New Testament Readings from Galatians 3:26—4:7; Roman 8:14-28

Responsive Reading from John 14:1-4

Reader:	Do not let your hearts be troubled.
Response:	**Believe in God, believe also in me.**
Reader:	In my Father's house there are many dwelling places.
Response:	**If it were not so, would I have told you that I go to prepare a place for you?**
Reader:	And if I go and prepare a place for you, I will come again and will take you to myself,
Response:	**So that where I am, there you may be also.**

Meditation and Prayer

Reading from John 13:33-35

A Time for Sharing

Comfort for the Living

Responsive Reading from Matthew 18:3-5, 10, Mark 10:14-16

Leader: Jesus loved the little children. Jesus loves us. He willingly gave his life for us. Jesus reminds us that we must have faith like a child, not only a child of God, but a small child who does not doubt or question, but who accepts God's Word and salvation.

Reader: Truly I tell you, unless you change and become like children, you will never enter the kingdom of heaven.

Response: Whoever becomes humble like this child is the greatest in the kingdom of heaven.

Reader: Whoever welcomes one such child in my name welcomes me. Take care that you do not despise one of these little ones;

Response: For, I tell you, in heaven their angels continually see the face of my Father in heaven.

Reader: Let the little children come to me; do not stop them;

Response: For it is to such as these that the kingdom of God belongs.

Reader: Truly I tell you, whoever does not receive the kingdom of God as a little child will never enter it.

Response: And he took them up in his arms, laid his hands on them, and blessed them.

The Lord's Prayer

All: Our Father which art in heaven, hallowed be thy name. Thy kingdom come. Thy will be done in earth, as it is in heaven. Give us this day our daily bread. And forgive us our debts, as we forgive our debtors. And lead us not into temptation, but deliver us from evil: For thine is the kingdom, and the power, and the glory, for ever. Amen.

Closing Prayer

Our Wounds Are Healed

(Family and friends are called to silence for the opening of the prayer service.)

Opening Invocation

Leader: In the name of the Father and the Son and the Holy Spirit. Amen.

He himself bore our sins in his body on the cross, so that, free from sins, we might live for righteousness; by his wounds you have been healed (1 Peter 2:24).

We are gathered here to celebrate the victory over death that _____ whose earthly sickness, sins, and scars have been healed by the death and resurrection of our Lord, Jesus Christ, the Great Healer.

After the people of that place recognized him, they sent word throughout the region and brought all who were sick to him, and begged him that they might touch even the fringe of his cloak; and all who touched it were healed (Matthew 14:35-36).

Responsive Reading from Psalm 30:1-2, 4-5

Reader: I will extol you, O Lord, for you have drawn me up,

Response: And did not let my foes rejoice over me.

Reader: O Lord my God, I cried to you for help,

Response: And you have healed me.

Reader: Sing praises to the Lord, O you his faithful ones,

Response: And give thanks to his holy name.

Reader: For his anger is but for a moment; his favor is for a lifetime.

Response: Weeping may linger for the night, but joy comes with the morning.

Prayer

Leader: Let us pray. Father, you have promised us eternal life through your Son, Jesus Christ. Through his wounds, we find healing on earth and in heaven. We thank you for this immeasurable gift. You have given us the Holy Spirit, the Comforter, and though our tears flow, you dry them with the joy of our salvation. Amen.

Old Testament Responsive Reading from Isaiah 58:8-11

Reader: Then your light shall break forth like the dawn, and your healing shall spring up quickly;

Response: Your vindicator shall go before you, the glory of the Lord shall be your rear guard.

Reader: Then you shall call, and the Lord will answer; you shall cry for help,

Response: And he will say, Here I am.

Reader: If you remove the yoke from among you, the pointing of the finger, the speaking of evil, if you offer your food to the hungry and satisfy the needs of the afflicted,

Response: Then your light shall rise in the darkness and your gloom be like the noonday.

Reader: The Lord will guide you continually, and satisfy your needs in parched places, and make your bones strong;

Response: And you shall be like a watered garden, like a spring of water, whose waters never fail.

New Testament Reading from Acts 4:8-12; Mark 5:38-42

Leader: God heals our wounds of body and spirit. In the gift of God's Son, Jesus, our healing is made complete, for we have been offered perfection through our salvation. We hear this from Peter in Acts 4:8-12:

Rulers of the people and elders, if we are questioned today because of a good deed done to someone who was sick and are asked how this man has been healed, let it be known to all of you, and to all the people of Israel, that this man is standing before you in good health by the name of Jesus Christ of Nazareth, whom you crucified, whom God raised from the dead. This Jesus is "the stone that was rejected by you, the builders; it has become the cornerstone." There is salvation in no one else, for there is no other name under heaven given among mortals by which we must be saved.

The Gospels record many miracles of healing. Touching the hem of Jesus' garments gave sight to the blind, hearing to the deaf, mobility to the paralyzed and lame, sanity to those filled with demons. The Gospel of Mark records a greater miracle, the raising of a child from death to life. We see these miracles as a foreshadowing of Jesus' ultimate purpose on earth, our salvation, by offering us life after death. We read in Mark 5:38-42:

When they came to the house of the leader of the synagogue, [Jesus] saw a commotion, people weeping and wailing loudly. When he had entered, he said to them, "Why do you make a commotion and weep? The child is not dead but sleeping." And they laughed at him. Then he put them all outside, and took the child's father and mother and those who were with him, and went in where the child was. He took her by the hand and said to her, "Talitha cum," which means, "Little girl, get up!" And immediately the girl got up and began to walk about (she was twelve years of age). At this they were overcome with amazement.

Responsive Reading from Isaiah 53:3-5

Reader: He was despised and rejected by others; a man of suffering and acquainted with infirmity;

Response: And as one from whom others hide their faces he was despised, and we held him of no account.

Reader: Surely he has borne our infirmities and carried our diseases;

Response: Yet we accounted him stricken, struck down by God, and afflicted.

109

Reader: But he was wounded for our transgressions, crushed for our iniquities;

Response: **Upon him was the punishment that made us whole, and by his bruises we are healed.**

Meditation and Prayer

Leader: In his suffering and death, Jesus gave us life. Let us reflect on the readings we heard a few moments ago. (*Silence*) Let us pray. Almighty God, you look over us in our frailty, pain, and sorrow, and you give us healing here on earth. We thank you, Heavenly Father, for giving us your Son, wounded and stricken for our sins, so that we may be healed from sin and death and have a home with you in heaven. In his name we pray. Amen.

Reading from Luke 6:18-23, 27-28, 31

Reader: They had come to hear him and to be healed of their diseases; and those who were troubled with unclean spirits were cured. And all in the crowd were trying to touch him, for power came out from him and healed all of them. Then he looked up at his disciples and said:

"Blessed are you who are poor, for yours is the kingdom of God. Blessed are you who are hungry now, for you will be filled. Blessed are you who weep now, for you will laugh. Blessed are you when people hate you, and when they exclude you, revile you, and defame you on account of the Son of Man. Rejoice in that day and leap for joy, for surely your reward is great in heaven; for that is what their ancestors did to the prophets. But I say to you that listen, Love your enemies, do good to those who hate you, bless those who curse you, pray for those who abuse you. Do to others as you would have them do to you."

Leader: Jesus reminds us in the reading we just heard that we are to "Love our enemies" and "Do to others as you would have them do to you." We know this is difficult.

We may recall many examples of compassion, kindness, forgiveness, and love which _____ has offered to us. Let us take a moment of silence of think of ways in which _____ touched our lives. (*Silence*) Now I will ask the family and friends if there are any memories or thoughts that you would like to share with those of us here.

A Time for Sharing
(*The leader will allow time for recollections.*)

Comfort for the Living
Reader: *For thus says the high and lofty one who inhabits eternity, whose name is Holy: I dwell in the high and holy place, and also with those who are contrite and humble in spirit, to revive the spirit of the humble, and to revive the heart of the contrite. I have seen their ways, but I will heal them; I will lead them and repay them with comfort, creating for their mourners the fruit of the lips. Peace, peace, to the far and the near, says the Lord; and I will heal them* (Isaiah 57:15, 18-19).

Responsive Reading from Ecclesiastes 3:1-4, 11
Reader: For everything there is a season,
Response: And a time for every matter under heaven:
Reader: A time to be born, and a time to die;
Response: A time to plant, and a time to pluck up what is planted;
Reader: A time to kill, and a time to heal;
Response: A time to break down, and a time to build up;
Reader: A time to weep, and a time to laugh;
Response: A time to mourn, and a time to dance.
All: He has made everything suitable for its time.
Leader: Let us pray the prayer that our Lord taught us:
All: Our Father which art in heaven, hallowed be thy name. Thy kingdom come. Thy will be done in earth, as it is in heaven. Give us this day our daily bread.

And forgive us our debts, as we forgive our debtors. And lead us not into temptation, but deliver us from evil: For thine is the kingdom, and the power, and the glory, for ever. Amen.

Closing Prayer

Leader: *I am weary with my moaning; every night I flood my bed with tears; I drench my couch with my weeping. My eyes waste away because of grief; they grow weak because of all my foes. Depart from me, all you workers of evil, for the Lord has heard the sound of my weeping. The Lord has heard my supplication; the Lord accepts my prayer* (Psalm 6:6-9).

Heavenly Father, you look into our hearts and offer comfort and peace to those who mourn. "You heal the brokenhearted and bind their wounds." Daily, we taste the fruits of our lives — war, peace, riches, poverty, joy, sorrow, life, and death. Help us to remember that each has its season. Teach us to accept the fruits of our days. We go in confidence that _____ lives with you in heaven. We thank you for your healing hand and for the gift you have given us, Jesus Christ, our Great Healer, in whose name we pray. Amen.

(The service is concluded.)

Our Wounds Are Healed

(The participants will read the portions of the service marked with
Response *and* **All.***)*

Opening Invocation

Responsive Reading from Psalm 30:1-2, 4-5
Reader: I will extol you, O Lord, for you have drawn me up,
Response: **And did not let my foes rejoice over me.**
Reader: O Lord my God, I cried to you for help,
Response: **And you have healed me.**
Reader: Sing praises to the Lord, O you his faithful ones,
Response: **And give thanks to his holy name.**
Reader: For his anger is but for a moment; his favor is for a
              lifetime.
Response: **Weeping may linger for the night, but joy comes
            with the morning.**

Prayer

Old Testament Responsive Reading from Isaiah 58:8-11
Reader: Then your light shall break forth like the dawn, and
              your healing shall spring up quickly;
Response: **Your vindicator shall go before you, the glory of
            the Lord shall be your rear guard.**
Reader: Then you shall call, and the Lord will answer; you
              shall cry for help,
Response: **And he will say, Here I am.**
Reader: If you remove the yoke from among you, the pointing
              of the finger, the speaking of evil, if you offer your
              food to the hungry and satisfy the needs of the afflicted,
Response: **Then your light shall rise in the darkness and your
            gloom be like the noonday.**

Reader: The Lord will guide you continually, and satisfy your needs in parched places, and make your bones strong;

Response: And you shall be like a watered garden, like a spring of water, whose waters never fail.

New Testament Reading from Acts 4:8-12; Mark 5:38-42

Responsive Reading from Isaiah 53:3-5

Reader: He was despised and rejected by others; a man of suffering and acquainted with infirmity;

Response: And as one from whom others hide their faces he was despised, and we held him of no account.

Reader: Surely he has borne our infirmities and carried our diseases;

Response: Yet we accounted him stricken, struck down by God, and afflicted.

Reader: But he was wounded for our transgressions, crushed for our iniquities;

Response: Upon him was the punishment that made us whole, and by his bruises we are healed.

Meditation and Prayer

Reading from Luke 6:18-23, 27-28, 31

A Time for Sharing

Comfort for the Living

Responsive Reading from Ecclesiastes 3:1-4, 11

Reader: For everything there is a season,

Response: And a time for every matter under heaven:

Reader: A time to be born, and a time to die;

Response: A time to plant, and a time to pluck up what is planted;

Reader: A time to kill, and a time to heal;

Response: A time to break down, and a time to build up;

Reader: A time to weep, and a time to laugh;
Response: A time to mourn, and a time to dance.
All: He has made everything suitable for its time.

The Lord's Prayer
All: Our Father which art in heaven, hallowed be thy name. Thy kingdom come. Thy will be done in earth, as it is in heaven. Give us this day our daily bread. And forgive us our debts, as we forgive our debtors. And lead us not into temptation, but deliver us from evil: For thine is the kingdom, and the power, and the glory, for ever. Amen.

Closing Prayer